INQUIRY-BASED
LESSONS
IN U.S. HISTORY

INQUIRY-BASED LESSONS IN U.S. HISTORY

Jana Kirchner, Ph.D., &
Andrew McMichael, Ph.D.

PRUFROCK PRESS INC.
WACO, TEXAS

Prufrock Press Inc.
P.O. Box 8813
Waco, TX 76714-8813
Phone: (800) 998-2208
Fax: (800) 240-0333
http://www.prufrock.com

TABLE OF CONTENTS

CHAPTER 1

INTRODUCTION

WHY WRITE THIS BOOK?

"How do I find primary sources that go along with my textbook?"

"Where do I locate political cartoons and maps that are appropriate for middle school students?"

"I want to use primary sources, but I don't have time to find good ones that fit in my units."

"I know I need to integrate literacy skills, but I don't know how with all this content to teach."

These are the types of questions and comments that United States history teachers at all grade levels have asked during our 10 years of working with three U.S. Department of Education Teaching American History (TAH) grants. While designing and implementing TAH grants with more than 200 elementary, middle, and high school teachers, we developed lessons that model teaching U.S. history through an inquiry format, with an essential question and primary sources for students to examine. This book is the culminating product of those professional development sessions, planning and coaching conferences with teachers, and site visits to watch inquiry-based, primary source lessons with students.

We have targeted the lessons in this book at middle school students, as that is often the first time that United States history is taught as a stand-alone subject rather than within an existing social studies course. The lessons in this book, however, would also be appropriate as lesson extensions for elementary students gifted in social studies, as supplemental history lessons to use in pull-out programs for advanced students, or for home-schooled students studying American history. Finally, although the target audience is middle school students, the lessons can easily be adapted for high school students as well.

INQUIRY IN SOCIAL STUDIES: UNDERSTANDING THE STANDARDS

At the time of publication, the focus in social studies is on the *College, Career, and Civic Life (C3) Framework* (National Council for the Social Studies [NCSS], 2013). Published in 2013 by a team of social studies professionals—curriculum specialists, K–12 teachers, social studies organizations, and university professors—from across the United States, the *C3 Framework* has been referred to as a "watershed moment for social studies education in America" (Herczog, 2013). The authors based the development of the *C3 Framework* on the following guiding principles about high-quality social studies instruction:

- Social studies prepares the nation's young people for college, careers, and civic life.
- Inquiry is at the heart of social studies.
- Social studies involves interdisciplinary applications and welcomes integration of the arts and humanities.
- Social studies is composed of deep and enduring understandings, concepts, and skills from the disciplines. Social studies emphasizes skills and practices as preparation for democratic decision-making.
- Social studies education should have direct and explicit connections to the Common Core State Standards for English Language Arts and Literacy in History/Social Studies. (Herczog, 2013, p. viii)

The foundation of the *C3 Framework* is its focus on the inquiry arc using four dimensions:

1. Developing Questions and Planning Inquiries
2. Applying Disciplinary Concepts and Tools
3. Evaluating Sources and Using Evidence

4. Communicating Conclusions and Taking Informed Action (NCSS, 2013).

Dimension 1 focuses on teachers or students creating compelling and supporting questions to frame a unit or lesson, and then determining helpful sources to answer that question. This dimension guided the lesson plan organization for this book as each lesson begins with an organizing question. In each lesson, teachers present the organizing question to their students; however, allowing students to generate their own questions is also an effective inquiry strategy. Dimension 2 targets the four content areas of civics, economics, geography, and history as "lenses students use in their inquiries" (NCSS, 2013, p. 29). This book focuses on history content and skills through student exploration of the story of United States history. Dimension 3, evaluating sources and evidence, includes gathering and evaluating sources, developing claims, and using evidence. Each lesson requires students to read and analyze a variety of primary sources as evidence that they will use to answer the organizing question. Dimension 4 involves students communicating and critiquing conclusions. Although the lessons in this book require students to develop a hypothesis and share it with the class, teachers ultimately have the flexibility to plan how the communication of conclusions will occur (i.e., the product for the lesson).

Gerwin and Zevin (2011) described the teacher's role in teaching history through inquiry as follows:

> First of all, encourage students to learn how to draw their own conclusions, and defend themselves against criticisms from other "detectives." Each participant, in effect, becomes a partner, a team member, in an investigation to which all have a chance to contribute. And contributions, including your own, must be defended and supported by evidence, sources, references, and reasons. You can join in with more suggestions, questions, and pointers, but this must be done carefully so as not to destroy students' sense of independent inquiry. (p. 21)

To successfully implement the lessons in this book, teachers must develop a classroom environment based in inquiry. Wineburg, Martin, and Monte-Sano (2013) expressed the importance of historical inquiry for 21st-century learners in this authentic way:

> In an age where 'I found it on the Internet' masquerades as knowledge, history serves as a vital counterweight to intellectual sloppiness. When a video uploaded from a cellphone in Tehran reaches San Francisco in

half a second, history reminds us to start with basic questions: Who sent it? Can it be trusted? What angle did the Flip Video miss? (p. ix)

The teacher is no longer the provider of knowledge but rather the facilitator of historical thinking. The strategies used in the lessons in this book help teachers achieve this.

Although the C3 foundational principles and the four dimensions of the inquiry arc are embedded in every lesson in this book, we chose to use the National Center for History in the Schools (NCHS; n.d.) standards for United States history (grades 5–12) as the source for specific content standards. At the time of publication of this book, individual states are developing social studies standards targeting the C3 Framework. The NCHS standards provide a common, national set of history standards that are often referenced in the social studies field.

Each chapter also includes the targeted Common Core State Standards (CCSS; National Governors Association Center for Best Practices & Council of Chief State School Officers, 2010) for Literacy in History/Social Studies appropriate for grades 6–8. Historical inquiry requires students to assemble information and draw conclusions from a variety of primary and secondary sources, which is the focus of the literacy standards. In describing this reading process, Wineburg, Martin, and Monte-Sano (2013) noted that "Historians have developed powerful ways of reading that allow them to see patterns, make sense of contradictions, and formulate reasoned interpretations . . . " (p. ix). With this focus on disciplinary literacy, or reading and thinking like a historian, the lessons in this book integrate multiple primary sources, including letters, journals, political cartoons, artwork, interviews, posters, pamphlets, and maps to encourage the students to do historical inquiry. The concept of "thinking like a historian" frames the way the lessons are created with a historical question, analyzing the evidence, creating a hypothesis, and using the specific evidence to support the hypothesis.

USING THE BOOK

We designed the lesson plans to align with the scope and sequence of a typical United States history course so that teachers can use them in several ways. First, teachers can use the lessons individually, tailoring them to local state standards and existing classroom curricula. Second, the lessons are also structured so that they can be used in a complementary fashion at appropriate places within the larger unit topic. Finally, teachers can swap out primary sources in each lesson with sources that they might already be using in their classrooms.

The chapters in this volume follow a similar structure. Each begins with a short essay on detailing the historical context to provide teachers with a reference point for the primary source materials in the lesson plans. Next, we list the NCHS United States history standards as well as the CCSS for Literacy in History/Social Studies targeted in the lessons. Following that introduction, each chapter contains three lessons.

We have divided each lesson into several parts, beginning with an organizing question that helps frame the lesson and the teaching strategies employed in the lesson. Each lesson also lists the primary source materials and web links to easily locate them. Depending on the ability of the students, teachers can use the entire primary source or choose their own excerpts. In some cases, the authors have provided excerpts within the lessons.

The lessons each follow a similar structure focused on students doing inquiry—thinking and reading like a historian. We developed individual lessons based on these phases: Lesson Hook, The Organizing Question, Examine the Sources, and Making a Hypothesis. Each part of the lesson includes detailed instructions for planning and implementing the lesson. The teaching strategies section in each of the lessons includes commonly used literacy strategies. Background information and tips for implementing these strategies are available from many online sources.

AN EXPLANATION OF THE SOURCES USED IN THE BOOK

This book uses many different types of primary sources to engage students. Some of the most common are photographs, cartoons, maps, and political writings. In cases where the lesson worked best with the original document, we provide a link to a stable website where teachers can easily locate the primary source. In cases where the lesson required an extract of the document, we have provided that.

Documents created at the time in which the event they portrayed occurred can sometimes be difficult to understand and interpret. Likewise, some of the more complex symbolism on some of the maps, for instance, might be too intricate for even the most advanced middle school child. However, all of the sources can be understood to some degree or another by all children. We chose the sources with the intent that each one has something for any child, regardless of current achievement level. For example, Johann Baptist Homann's map in Chapter 4 is rich with multilayered symbolism, some of which continues to elude even professional historians. Nonetheless, this is a lesson we have used with hundreds of schoolchildren in elementary and middle schools with great success—all children can find something.

The original language in some of the documents can seem strange to 21st-century readers. People did not always use modern spellings, and in many cases there was no standard way to spell a word. In cases where the original English was too difficult, we have updated the language to modern English and indicated such on the text. In cases where the original English was archaic, or contained misspellings, but was still readable, we have left the writing intact but acknowledged the misspellings in the original with [sic].

SIMPLE SEARCH TIPS FOR FINDING OTHER SOURCES

Finding additional primary sources to use with these and other lesson plans is as easy as turning to Google and keeping in mind a few search tips and tricks. The most important thing to remember is that Google returns the results it thinks you want, not necessarily the ones you actually want. To get the search engine to return useful results, it helps to narrow the search parameters using some simple modifier commands. For example, the plus (+) and minus (-) signs will force the engine to either include or exclude certain terms. So the search in Figure 1.1 will force Google to return only those results that contain the word colony along with Jamestown, while the search in Figure 1.2 will return the same results but without any pages that mention Pocahontas. It often helps to narrow the search to those sites with more reliable collections of sources, and using Google is almost always easier than a website's search engine. So the search in Figure 1.3 will only show results from the Library of Congress online collections that contain the exact phrase "civil war." A search like that in Figure 1.4 brings up results from the American Memory collection at the Library of Congress. Clicking on Google's "Images" tab brings up the vast collection of images there. When downloading from that site, be aware that clicking on the "jpeg" or "tif" images brings up a higher resolution version but also takes longer to download.

Sometimes the simplest search is the best way to begin. When looking for primary sources on the American Revolution, the search in Figure 1.5 turns up more than 200,000 results. From there, the search box can be modified with the insertion of +jefferson, site:loc.gov, or any of the above-mentioned modifiers.

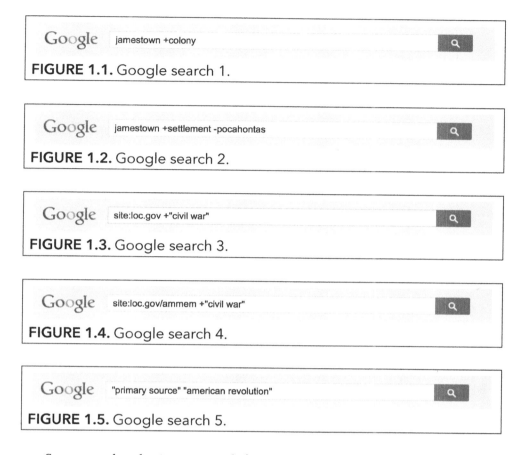

FIGURE 1.1. Google search 1.

FIGURE 1.2. Google search 2.

FIGURE 1.3. Google search 3.

FIGURE 1.4. Google search 4.

FIGURE 1.5. Google search 5.

Some very handy sites to search for primary sources are:
- The Library of Congress (http://www.loc.gov)
- The National Archives (http://www.archives.gov)
- The Internet Archive's Prelinger Archives (http://www.archive.org/details/prelinger)
- The Internet History Sourcebooks Project (http://www.fordham.edu/halsall)
- The Avalon Project (http://www.avalon.law.yale.edu)

Google can help find more, with a search on "primary source sites" (without the quotes) returning more than 4.4 million hits and "primary source websites" (again without the quotes) returning more than 900,000.

LIFE BEFORE 1600

CHAPTER 2

LIFE BEFORE 1600
COLLISION OF CULTURES

Presently we saw several of the natives advancing towards our party, and one of them came up to us, to whom we gave some hawk's bells and glass beads, with which he was delighted . . . I shall depart immediately, if the weather serve, and sail round the island, till I succeed in meeting with the king, in order to see if I can acquire any of the gold, which I hear he possesses.–Christopher Columbus, Journal Entry, October 21, 1492

HISTORICAL BACKGROUND: WHAT DO I NEED TO KNOW?

After returning from the Crusades with exotic goods from the Middle East and Asia, Europeans began searching for a sea route to Asia, starting down the coast of Africa in the late 14th century. The Africa they encountered was a land of dozens of sophisticated kingdoms and hundreds of ethnic groups, each with distinct and separate cultures and languages. African kingdoms and peoples north of the Sahara Desert largely practiced Islam and had regular contact with Europeans and the Middle East. First contacts along the central and south coast opened up an African trade in precious metals, cloth, ivory, and other luxury items. Coastal African kingdoms also sold African slaves captured in war, initiating what would become a well-established trade.

The Americas in the 15th century similarly contained an array of nations and peoples who spoke hundreds of mutually unintelligible languages. In the same way as African and European kingdoms, Native American kingdoms and towns maintained extensive trade routes, waged war against each other, and used diplomacy in support of alliances. Like most African nations, Native American peoples regarded land as something that could be used for a time, but that was not subject to permanent ownership in the European sense of the word. So, land could not be "bought" or "sold," but could be controlled by one group or another. Although it is difficult to generalize, most Native Americans and central and southern Africans held similar religious beliefs, called animism, in which spirits inhabited physical objects and in which there was an overall creator-deity.

In both cultures, a singular chief or king ruled over a population with a clear division of labor between men and women. In Native societies that relied on hunting large animals for food, that task usually went to men, while women gathered food and produced clothing. In native societies that practiced agriculture, unlike Europeans, families were defined through a female line of descent. In most Native American cultures, political power was divided between civil and military leaders who had authority only so long as they had the support of their people. Autocratic power of the kind Europeans were used to was unusual.

The European quest for riches in Asia eventually led Christopher Columbus to embark on a journey across the Atlantic. Upon landing, with his men on the verge of revolt, Columbus claimed to have "discovered" islands off the coast of Japan, or possibly China, or even India. In reality he was in what is now called the Caribbean and made contact with the Carib, Taino, and Arawak Indians. Subsequent explorers also discovered native civilizations rich with gold, setting off a frenzy of exploration and exploitation. During the 16th century, Spain shipped back so much gold that the resulting inflation caused problems with the European economy.

England, consumed with wars and internal dynastic struggles during the 16th century, observed these changes with a growing sense of alarm. Advocates of English expansion wrote with urgency about England's need to send ships and establish colonies. Some of these writers, Richard Hakluyt among them, had never visited the Americas and instead gathered second- and third-hand information. Thomas Hariot's report was the first written by an Englishman who had been to North America. Both accounts made a deep impression on the English Crown, prompting a wave of exploration and settlement that began in the early 17th century, more than 100 years after the first Spanish settlements.

STANDARDS ADDRESSED

National Council for History in the Schools (NCHS) U.S. History Content Standards, Grades 5–12 (available at http://www.nchs.ucla.edu/history-standards/us-history-content-standards):

- Comparative characteristics of societies in the Americas, Western Europe, and Western Africa that increasingly interacted after 1450
- How early European exploration and colonization resulted in cultural and ecological interactions among previously unconnected peoples

Common Core State Standards (CCSS) for Literacy in History/Social Studies, Grades 6–8 (available at http://www.corestandards.org/ELA-Literacy/):

- Cite specific textual evidence to support analysis of primary and secondary sources.
- Distinguish among fact, opinion, and reasoned judgment in a text.

LESSON 1

ORGANIZING QUESTION

What was life like in a Powhatan village?

STRATEGIES USED

Mystery Strategy, Cooperative Learning

MATERIALS NEEDED

1. One copy of Clue Sheet: Life in a Powhatan Village for each student (**Handout 2.1**)
2. Chart paper and markers for each group of three to five students
3. One copy of each primary source placed in stations around the room. The following engravings are by Theodor de Bry (ca. 1570–1590), after drawings by John White. They can be found through the Jamestown-Yorktown Foundation at http://historyisfun.org/pdf/In-the-Words-of-Pocahontas/PIndians_Images.pdf. Students will also need the artifacts at the end of the list.
   - ✓ Engraving: "Their Manner of Feeding"
   - ✓ Engraving: "The Town of Secota"
   - ✓ Engraving: "Their Manner of Fishing in Virginia"
   - ✓ Engraving: "Their Manner of Making Boats"
   - ✓ Engraving: "The Broiling of Their Fish over the Flame"
   - ✓ Engraving: "A Werowan or Great Lorde of Virginia"
   - ✓ Engraving: "The Town of Pomeiooc"
   - ✓ First-Person Account: Excerpts From Gabriel Archer's (1607/1998) "A Brief Description of the People" (**Handout 2.2**)
   - ✓ Artifacts: blue beads, reed (raffia also works well), bones, leather strips, etc.

LESSON PLAN

Lesson Hook: As students enter the room, display a picture of an archaeology dig on the screen. Explain the following task to students:

Your help is needed with a very important historical project! The Association of the Preservation of Virginia Antiquities (APVA) has decided to hire archaeologists to study the Powhatan culture. You will be taking on the role of a team of archaeologists to examine clues posted around the room, to determine the answer to the question, and to report your findings to the APVA.

The Organizing Question: Explain that students' task is to examine the clues around the room, collect data on their clue sheet, and determine the answer to the question: What was life like in a Powhatan village?

Examine the Sources: *Cooperative Learning*—Divide students into groups of three to five, assigning each group member a role of Chief Archaeologist, Recorder, Reporter, Sketch Artist, and/or Project Manager. Discuss the duties of each role. Modify these roles and responsibilities as needed to fit the size of your groups and student needs.

Gallery Walk—Pass out the Clue Sheet: Life in a Powhatan Village (**Handout 2.1**) for data collection. Model one of the images at the stations with students so they can see how to analyze an image and collect the evidence on the clue sheet. Allow students time to view the images and artifacts, to take notes on their clue sheets, and to discuss the findings with their team.

Make a Hypothesis: Explain to the archaeology teams that they are to make a hypothesis about the Powhatan culture and use the chart paper and markers to provide a visual depiction of their hypothesis. Teams should be prepared to explain their hypothesis and visual depiction using evidence from the clues around the room. After students have been given adequate time, have groups present their posters to the class. If possible, have administrators or other teachers serve as members of the APVA board and make this a contest where the "board" votes for the most accurate and thorough presentation.

Depending on the thoroughness and content accuracy of the presentations, end this lesson with a discussion of misconceptions, what content might have been missing from the clues, and ways to find more information to answer the organizing question. Have them answer these questions individually as a formative assessment for the lesson:

- What are four details about Powhatan culture that you learned from this archaeology project?
- How was your hypothesis supported by the evidence or clues?
- How do you think this activity was similar to the job of a real archaeologist?
- How well did each group member perform the role he or she was assigned?

HANDOUT 2.1
CLUE SHEET: LIFE IN A POWHATAN VILLAGE

Directions: Using the clues around the room, collect evidence and take notes on the things you notice about daily life in a Powhatan village in the 17th century. Organize them into one of the categories at the bottom of the page. Use the evidence to form a hypothesis answering the question: What was life like in a Powhatan village?

Notes:			
Government	**Roles of Men**	**Roles of Women**	**Family Structure**
Trade	**Warfare**	**Food**	**Religious Beliefs**

Our hypothesis is:_____

_____

_____

The evidence to support this hypothesis is:_____

_____

_____

HANDOUT 2.2
EXCERPTS FROM GABRIEL ARCHER'S (1607/1998) "A BRIEF DESCRIPTION OF THE PEOPLE"

There is a king in this land called Great Pawatah, under whose dominion are at least 20 several kingdoms, yet each king potent as a prince in his own territory. These have their subjects at so quick command as a beck brings obedience, even to the restitution of stolen goods, which by their natural inclination they are loth to leave.

They go all naked save their privities, yet in cool weather they wear deerskins with the hair on the loose. Some have leather stockings up to their twists and sandals on their feet.

Their hair is black generally, which they wear long on the left side, tied up on a knot, about which knot the kings and best among them have a kind of coronet of deer's hair colored red. Some have chains of long link'd copper about their necks, and some chains of pearl. The common sort stick long feathers in this knot. I found not a gray eye among them all. Their skin is tawny, not so born but with dyeing and painting themselves, in which they delight greatly.

The women are like the men, only this difference: Their hair groweth long all over their heads, save clip'd somewhat short afore. These do all the labor, and the men hunt and go at their pleasure.

They live commonly by the waterside in little cottages made of canes and reeds, covered with the bark of trees. They dwell as I guess by families of kindred and alliance, some 40ty or 50ty in a hatto, or small village, which towns are not past a mile or half a mile asunder in most places.

They live upon sodden wheat, beans, and peas for the most part. Also they kill deer, take fish in their weirs, and kill fowl abundance. They eat often and that liberally.

They are proper lusty, straight men, very strong, run exceeding swiftly; their fight is always in the wood with bow and arrows, and a short wooden sword. The celerity they use in skirmish is admirable. The king directs the battle and is always in front.

Their manner of entertainment is upon mats on the ground under some tree, where they sit themselves alone in the middest of the mat, and two mats on each side, on which their people sit; then right against him (making a square form) sat we always. When they came to their mat they have an usher goes before them, and the rest as he sits down give a long shout.

They sacrifice tobacco to the sun, [a] fair picture, or a harmful thing (as a sword or a piece) also; they strinkle some into the water in the morning before they wash.

They have many wives, to whom, as I could perceive, they keep constant. The Great King Pawatah had most wives. These they abide not to be touch'd before their face.

The women are very cleanly in making their bread and preparing meat. I found they account after death to go into another world, pointing eastward to the element. And when they saw us at prayer they observed us with great silence and respect, especially those to whom I had imparted the meaning of our reverence.

To conclude, they are a very witty and ingenious people, apt both to understand and speak our language, so that I hope in God, as He hath miraculously preserved us hither from all dangers, both of sea and land and their fury, so He will make us authors of His holy will in converting them to our true Christian faith by His own inspiring grace and knowledge of His deity.

LESSON 2

ORGANIZING QUESTION

What happened when Columbus and Native Americans first encountered each other?

STRATEGIES USED

Picture Prediction

MATERIALS NEEDED

1. Painting: John Vanderlyn's (1847) *Landing of Columbus*, available at http://www.aoc.gov/capitol-hill/historic-rotunda-paintings/landing-columbus
2. Secondary Source: Jane Yolen's (1992) *Encounter*, a children's book available in most libraries
3. Journals: Three or four copies per group of a day's journal entry from Christopher Columbus' *Personal Narrative of the First Voyage of Columbus to America* (1820; translated from Spanish), available at https://archive.org/details/personalnarrativ00colu
   ✓ Group 1: October 11 (pp. 34–37)
   ✓ Group 2: October 13 (pp. 37–39)
   ✓ Group 3: October 14 (pp. 39–41)
   ✓ Group 4: October 17 (pp. 48–51)

LESSON PLAN

This lesson works well as an introduction to textbook chapters on exploration, clash of cultures, and empires in the Americas.

Lesson Hook: *Picture Prediction*—Show John Vanderlyn's (1847) *Landing of Columbus* from the U.S. Capitol Rotunda to the class. Ask students to examine the painting and respond to these two questions:
- What details do you notice in the painting?
- What might this visual predict about encounters between Columbus and Native Americans?

Prompt students to explain their predictions with details and evidence from the painting. Make a list of these predictions on the board.

Read Jane Yolen's (1992) *Encounter* to the class, showing the visuals in the book while reading. As students are listening, ask them to think about how this perspective compares and contrasts with the painting and share their thoughts.

The Organizing Question: Explain to students that they will read the journals of Columbus for clues to answer the organizing question: What happened when Columbus and Native Americans first encountered each other?

Examine the Sources: Explain that students will examine translations of Columbus's journals from his first voyage to the Americas. Before the activity begins, show a map of the voyage, explain the story of Ferdinand and Isabella, and tell them that Columbus referred to himself as "The Admiral" in these entries. Divide the class into four groups and give them each copies of a single day from the journal, as described in the "Materials Needed" section.

As they read their assigned journal entry, have them look for and underline examples of events that occurred in these first encounters between Columbus and the native people.

Make a Hypothesis: Using details from the journal entries, have each group write a hypothesis that answers the organizing question and share the hypothesis and evidence with the class. Encourage students to compare and contrast the events in Columbus's journals with the predictions they made from Vanderlyn's (1847) *Landing of Columbus* and the Taino perspective described in *Encounter* (Yolen, 1992).

LESSON 3

ORGANIZING QUESTION

How did Englishmen who had never been to the New World imagine North America?

STRATEGIES USED

Gist

MATERIALS NEEDED

1. One copy of each document for half of the class:
   ✓ Manuscript: Excerpts From Richard Hakluyt's (1584) *Discourse on Western Planting* (**Handout 2.3**), available at https://archive.org/details/cihm_07386
   ✓ Book: Excerpts From Thomas Hariot's (1590) A Brief and True Report of the New Found Land of Virginia (**Handout 2.4**), available at http://etext.lib.virginia.edu/etcbin/Jamestown-brosemod?id=J1009

2. One highlighter per student

LESSON PLAN

Lesson Hook: Display a picture of the moon on a screen as students enter class. Tell students the following:

> You have been given the job to set up a colony on the moon. You must figure out a way to get people to travel to the moon and live there. With a partner, make a list of all of the information about living on the moon that you would need to share with people and the advertising techniques you could use to get them to go on this journey.

As they work, prompt students with these questions: Why might people want to go? What techniques would you use to recruit them? What do you think are some factors that would make people want to relocate to a new city or country?

After a few minutes, ask students to share their ideas. List students' ideas and strategies on the board and guide their thinking with questions a "lunar colonist" might have. These could include safety, ease of travel, land, jobs, food available, types of houses, wealth, fame, adventure, good maps or directions about how to get there, and pictures of what colonists' new homes might look like.

The Organizing Question: Explain that they will examine two documents for clues to answer the organizing question: How did Englishmen who had never been to the New World imagine North America?

Examine the Sources: Provide students with background information on Richard Hakluyt's (1584) and Thomas Hariot's (1590) works. Divide the class into groups of three—half of the groups should get the Hakluyt document (**Handout 2.3**) and the other half should get the Hariot one (**Handout 2.4**). Because of its length, the Hariot source is chunked into four sections (trade items, food, animals, and people), so the groups with that source can be assigned only one of the sections or chunks.

   Gist—Tell students that they will be reading the documents and using the Gist strategy. As one group member reads each section of the document, a second group member should write in the margin the Gist, or summary, of what it means in five words or less. The third group member should use a highlighter to mark examples of evidence that might make people want to travel to the Americas, such as goods, trade items, or land. Model one section from the documents as an example of what students should do in this task. Groups should stop at the end of each section to discuss their Gist words and highlighted evidence. At the end of each document discussion, students should be ready to share answers to these questions with the class:
   - What evidence from your document shows incentives to persuade people to go to the New World?
   - How did Hakluyt or Hariot use promotional techniques or language to accomplish this?

While students are sharing their responses, provide examples of what was going on back in Europe that would make the examples from documents interesting to travelers.

Make a Hypothesis: Ask students to use the lesson hook and the two handouts to answer the organizing question. End the lesson with a summary discussion or an exit slip assessment of the reasons people came to the Americas and techniques that were used to promote colonization and settlement. Make sure students cite evidence from each primary source to support their hypotheses.

HANDOUT 2.3
EXCERPTS FROM RICHARD HAKLUYT'S
DISCOURSE ON WESTERN PLANTING

Richard Hakluyt (1584) was an English writer who advocated for exploration and settlement in North America. His first work, in 1582, *Divers Voyages Touching the Discoverie of America*, was based on interviews with sailors, some of whom had been to the Americas. His advocacy for English supremacy contained nationalist, political, economic, and religious arguments highlighting existing tensions with Spain, one of England's chief competitors on the world stage.

Original	Translation
That this Westerne discoverie will be greately for thinlargemente of the gospell of Christe.	Ch. 1: That this western discovery will be greatly for the enlargement of the gospel of Christ.
That all other Englishe trades are growen beggarly or daungerous, especially daungerous in all the Kinge of Spayne his domynions.	Ch. 2: That all other English trades are grown beggarly or dangerous, especially dangerous in all the King of Spain his dominions.
That this westerne voyadge will yelde unto us all the commodities of Europe, Affrica and Asia, as far as wee were wonte to travell, and supplye the wantes of all our decayed trades.	Ch. 3: That this western voyage will yield unto us all the commodities of Europe, Africa, and Asia, as far as we were wont to travel, and supply the wants of all our decayed trades.
That this enterprizo will be for the manifolde ymployment of nombers of idle men.	Ch. 4: That this enterprise will be for the manifold employment of numbers of idle men.
That the Spainardes have exercised moste outrageous . . . cruelties in all the West Indies . . . whoe woulde joyne with us . . . willinglye to shake of their moste intollerable yoke.	Ch. 11: That the Spaniards have exercised most outrageous . . . cruelties in all the West Indies . . . who would join with us [and] . . . willingly shake off their most intolerable yoke.
That the passage in this voyadge is easie and shorte, that it cutteth not nere the trade of any other mightie princes, no nere their contries, that it is to be performed at all times of the yere.	Ch. 12: That the passage in this voyage is easy and short, that it cuts not near the trade of any other mighty princes, nor near their countries, that it is to be performed at all times of the year.
That hereby the revenewes and customes of her Majestie, bothe outewarde and inwarde, shall mightely be inlarged by the toll, excises, and other dueties which withoute oppression may be raysed.	Ch. 13: That hereby the revenues and customs of her Majesty, both outward and inward, shall mightily be enlarged by the toll, excises, and other duties which without oppression may be raised.
That this action will be for the greate increase, mayneteynaunce, and safetie of our navie, and especially of great shippinge, which is the strengthe of our realme, and for the supportation of all those occupations that depende upon the same.	Ch. 14: That this action will be for the great increase, maintenance, and safety of our navy, and especially of great shipping, which is the strength of our realm, and for the support of all those occupations that depend on the same.
That by these colonies the north west passage to Cathaio and China may easily, quickly, and perfectly be searched oute as well by river and overlande as by the sea.	Ch. 17: That by these colonies the northwest passage to Cathay and China may easily, quickly, and perfectly be searched out as well by river and overland as by the sea.
That the Queene of Englandes title to all the West Indies, or at the leaste to as muche as is from Florida to the Circle articke, is more lawfull and righte then the Spaniardes, or any other Christian Princes.	Ch. 18: That the Queen of England's title to all the West Indies, or at the least to as much as is from Florida to the Arctic Circle, is more lawful and right than the Spaniards', or any other Christian Princes'.

HANDOUT 2.4
EXCERPTS FROM THOMAS HARIOT'S
(1590) *A BRIEF AND TRUE REPORT OF THE NEW FOUND LAND OF VIRGINIA*

THE FIRST PART, OF MERCHANTABLE COMMODITIES

SILK OF GRASS OR GRASS SILK

There is a kind of grass in the country upon the blades where of there grows very good silk in form of a thin glittering skin to be stript off. It grows two foot and a half high or better: the blades are about two foot in length, and half inch broad. The like grows in Persia, which is in the self same climate as Virginia, of which very many of the silk works that come from thence into Europe are made. Here of if it be planted and ordered as in Persia, it cannot in reason be otherwise, but that there will rise in short time great profit to the dealers therein; seeing there is so great use and vent thereof as well in our country as elsewhere. And by the means of sowing and planting in good ground, it will be far greater, better, and more plentiful than it is. Although notwithstanding there is great store thereof in many places of the country growing naturally and wild. Which also by proof here in England, in making a piece of silk Grosgrain, we found to be excellent good.

WORME SILK

In many of our journeys we found silk worms fair and great; as big as our ordinary walnuts. Although it has not been our hap to have found such plenty as elsewhere to be in the country we have heard of; yet seeing that the country does naturally breed and nourish them, there is no doubt but if art be added in planting of mulberry trees and others fit for them in commodious places, for their feeding and nourishing; and some of them carefully gathered and husbanded in that fort as by men of skill is known to be necessary: there will rise as great profit in time to the Virginians, as thereof does now to the Persians, Turks, Italians and Spaniards.

CEDAR

Cedar, a very sweet wood and fine timber; whereof if nests of chests be there made, or timber thereof fitted for sweet and fine bedsteads, tables, desks, lutes, virginals and many things else, (of which there has been proof made already) to make up freight with other principal commodities will yield profit.

WINE

There are two kinds of grapes that the soil does yield naturally: the one is small and sour of the ordinary bigness as ours in England: the other far greater and of himself luscious sweet. When they are planted and husbanded as they ought, a principal commodity of wines by them may be raised.

HANDOUT 2.4, CONTINUED

OYLE

There are two sorts of Walnuts both holding oil, but the one far more plentiful than the other. When there are mills and other devices for the purpose, a commodity of them may be raised because there are infinite store. There are also three several kinds of Berries in the form of Oak acorns, which also by the experience and use of the inhabitants, we find to yield very good and sweet oil. Furthermore the *Bears* of the country are commonly very fat, and in some places there are many: their fatness because it is so liquid, may well be termed oil, and hath many special uses.

FURS

All along the Sea coast there are great store of Otters, which being taken by weirs and other engines made for the purpose, will yield good profit.

DEER SKINS

Deer skins dressed after the manner of Chamoes or undressed are to be had of the natural inhabitants thousands yearly by way of traffic for trifles: and no more waste or spoil of Deer than is and has been ordinarily in time before.

IRON

In two places of the country specially, one about fourscore and the other six score miles from the Fort or place where we dwelt: we found near the water side the ground to be rocky, which by the trial of a mineral man, was found to hold Iron richly. It is found in many places of the country else. I know nothing to the contrary, but that it may be allowed for a good merchantable commodity.

COPPER

A hundred and fifty miles into the mainland in two towns we found with the inhabitants diverse small plates of copper, that had been made as we understood, by the inhabitants that dwell farther into the country: where as they say are mountains and Rivers that yield also white grains of Metal, which is to be deemed Silver.

PEARL

Sometimes in feeding on mussels we found some pearl; but it was our hap to meet with rags, or of a pied colour; not having yet discovered those places where we heard of better and more plenty. One of our company; a man of skill in such matters, had gathered together from among the savage people about five thousand . . .

SUGAR CANES

We carried thither Sugar canes to plant which being not so well preserved as was requisite, and besides the time of the year being past for their setting when we arrived, we could not make that proof of them as we desired. Notwithstanding seeing that they grow in the same climate, in the South part of Spain and in Barbary, our hope in rea-

HANDOUT 2.4, CONTINUED

son may yet continue. So likewise for *Oranges* and *Lemons*, there may be planted also Quinces. Whereby may grow in reasonable time if the action be diligently prosecuted no small commodities in *Sugars*, *Sweetmeats*, and Marmalades.

THE SECOND PART, OF SUCH COMMODITIES AS VIRGINIA IS KNOWN TO YIELD FOR VICTUAL AND SUSTENANCE OF MAN'S LIFE, USUALLY FED UPON BY THE NATURAL INHABITANTS: AS ALSO BY US DURING THE TIME OF OUR ABODE.

PAGATOWR, a kind of grain so called by the inhabitants; the same in the West Indies is called MAIZE: English men call it Guinney wheat or Turkey wheat , according to the names of the countries from whence the like has been brought. The grain is about the bigness of our ordinary English peas and not much different in form and shape: but of diverse colors: some white, some red, some yellow, and some blue. All of them yield a very white and sweet flour: being used according to his kind it makes a very good bread. We made of the same in the country some malt, whereof was bewed as good ale as was to be desired. So likewise by the help of hops thereof may be made as good Beer.

Okindgier, called by us Beans, because in greatness and partly in shape they are like to be the Beans in England; saving that they are flatter, of more diverse colors, and some pied. The leaf also of the stem is much different. In taste they are altogether as good as our English peas.

Maccqwer, according to their several forms called by us, *Pumpkins*, *Mellons* , and *Gourds*, because they are of the like forms as those kinds in England. In *Virginia* such of several forms are of one taste and very good, and do also spring from one seed. There are two sorts; one is ripe in the space of a month, and the other in two months.

OF FRUITES

CHESTNUTS, there are in diverse places great store: some they use to eat raw, some they stamp and boil to make spoonmeat, and with some being sodden they make such a manner of dough bread as they use of their beans before mentioned.

WALNUTS: There are two kinds of Walnuts, and of then infinite store: In many places where very great woods for many miles together the third part of trees are walnut trees. The one kind is of the same taste and form or little differing from ours of England, but that they are harder and thicker shelled: the other is greater and has a very ragged and hard shell: but the kernel great, very oily and sweet.

METAQUESUNNAUK, a kind of pleasant fruit almost of the shape and bigness of English pears, but that they are of a perfect red color as well within as without.

GRAPES there are of two sorts which I mentioned in the merchantable commodities.

STRAWBERRIES there are as good and as great as those which we have in our English gardens.

MULBERRIES, Crab apples, Hurts or Whortleberries, such as we have in England.

HANDOUT 2.4, CONTINUED

OF BEASTS

Deer, in some places there are great store: near unto the sea coast they are of the ordinary bigness as ours in England, and some less: but further up into the country where there is better seed they are greater: they differ from ours only in this, their tails are longer and the snags of their horns look backward.

Coneys, Those that we have seen and all that we can hear of are of a grey color like unto hares: in some places there are such plenty that all the people of some towns make them mantles of the fur or net of the skins of those they usually take.

Saquenckot and *Maquwoc*, two kinds of small beasts greater than coneys which are very good meat. We never took any of them our selves, but sometime eat of such as the inhabitants had taken and brought unto us.

Squirrels which are of a grey color, we have taken and eaten.

Bears which are all of black color. The bears of this country are good meat; the inhabitants in time of winter do use to take and eat many, so also sometime did we.

OF FOWL

Turkey cocks and *Turkey hens*: Stockdoves: Partridges: *Cranes*: *Herns*: and in winter great store of *Swans* and *Geese*. Of all sorts of fowl I have the names in the country language of fourscore and six of which number besides those that be named, we have taken, eaten, and have the pictures as they were there drawn . . .

There are also *Parrots*, *Falcons*, and *Marlin hawks*, which although with us they be not used for meat, yet for other causes I thought good to mention.

OF FISHE

For four months of the year, February, March, April and May, there are plenty of *Sturgeons*: And also in the same months of Herrings, some of the ordinary bigness as ours in England, but the most part far greater, of eighteen, twenty inches, and some two foot in length and better; both these kinds of fish in those months are most plentiful, and in best season which we found to be most delicate and pleasant meat.

There are also *Trout*, Porpoises, *Rays*, *Oldwives*, *Mullets*, *Plaice*, and very many other sorts of excellent good fish, which we have taken and eaten . . .

Sea crabs, such as we have in England.

Oysters, some very great, and some small; some round and some of a long shape: They are found both in salt water and brackish, and those that we had out of salt water are far better than the other as in our own country.

Also *Mussels*, *Scallops*, Periwinkles, and Creuises.

There are many *Tortoises* both of land and sea kind, their backs and bellies are shelled very thick; their head, feet, and tail , which are in appearance, seem ugly as though they were members of a serpent or venemous: but notwithstanding they are very good meat, as also their eggs . Some have been found of a yard in breadth and better.

HANDOUT 2.4, CONTINUED

THE THIRD AND LAST PART, OF SUCH OTHER THINGS AS IS BEHOOFFULL FOR THOSE WHICH SHALL PLANT AND INHABIT TO KNOW OF; WITH A DESCRIPTION OF THE NATURE AND MANNERS OF THE PEOPLE OF THE COUNTRY.

OF THE NATURE AND MANNERS OF THE PEOPLE

It rests I speak a word or two of the natural inhabitants, their natures and manners, leaving large discourse thereof until time more convenient hereafter: now only so far forth, as that you may know, how that they in respect of troubling our inhabiting and planting, are not to be feared; but that they shall have cause both to fear and love us that shall inhabit with them.

They are a people clothed with loose mantles made of Deer skins, and aprons of the same round about their middles; all else naked; of such a difference of statures only as we in England; having no edge tools or weapons of iron or steel to offend us withal, neither know they how to make any: those weapons that they have, are only bows made of Witch hazel, and arrows of reeds; flat edged truncheons also of wood about a yard long, neither have they any thing to defend themselves but targets made of bark; and some armor made of sticks wickered together with thread.

Their towns are but small, and near the sea coast but few, some containing but 10 or 12 houses: some 20. The greatest that we have seen have been but of 30 houses: if they be walled it is only done with barks of trees made fast to stakes, or else with poles only fixed upright and close one by another.

Their houses are made of small poles made fast at the tops in round form after the manner as is used in many arbors in our gardens of England, in most towns covered with bark, and in some with artificial mats made of long rushes; from the tops of the houses down to the ground. The length of them is commonly double to the breadth, in some places they are but 12 and 16 yards long, and in other some we have seen of four and twenty.

If there fall out any wars between us and them, what their fight is likely to be, we having advantages against them so many manner of ways, as by our discipline, our strange weapons and devices else; especially by ordinance great and small, it may be easily imagined; by the experience we have had in some places, the turning up of their heels against us in running away was their best defense .

In respect of us they are a people poor, and for want of skill and judgment in the knowledge and use of our things, do esteem our trifles before things of greater value: Notwithstanding in their proper manner considering the want of such means as we have, they seem very ingenious; For although they have no such tools, nor any such crafts, sciences and arts as we; yet in those things they do, they show excellency of wit. And by how much they upon due consideration shall find our manner of knowledge and crafts to exceed theirs in perfection, and speed for doing or execution, by so much more the more is it probable that they should desire our friendships and love, and have the greater respect for pleasing and obeying us. Whereby may be hoped if means of

HANDOUT 2.4, CONTINUED

good government be used, that they may in short time be brought to civility, and the embracing of true religion.

Some religion they have already, which although it be far from the truth, yet being as it is, there is hope it may be the easier and sooner reformed.

Many times and in every town where I came, according as I was able, I made declaration of the contents of the Bible; that therein was set forth the true and only God, and his mighty works, that therein was contained the true doctrine of salvation through Christ, with many particularities of Miracles and chief points of religion, as I was able then to utter, and thought fit for the time. And although I told them the book materially and of itself was not of any such virtue, as I thought they did conceive, but only the doctrine therein contained; yet would many be glad to touch it, to embrace it, to kiss it, to hold it to their breasts and heads, and stroke over all their body with it; to show their hungry desire of that knowledge which was spoken of.

1607-1650

CHAPTER 3

SETTLING IN

> . . . Adventurers of and for our City of London, and all such others, as are, or shall be, joined unto them of that Colony, shall be called the first Colony; And they shall and may begin their said first Plantation and Habitation, at any Place upon the said-Coast of Virginia or America, where they shall think fit and convenient, between the said four and thirty and one and forty Degrees of the said Latitude; And that they shall have all the Lands, Woods, Soil, Grounds, Havens, Ports, Rivers, Mines, Minerals, Marshes, Waters, Fishings, Commodities . . . –King James I, The First Charter of Virginia, 1606

HISTORICAL BACKGROUND: WHAT DO I NEED TO KNOW?

Conditions in England prompted a migration in the 17th century. Widespread poverty brought more people to the cities, which became overcrowded. Disease and crime increased, the economic and social fabric of England began to strain, and more people felt the need to leave England—colonists were almost always pushed by the situation in their home countries, rather than pulled by the possibilities at their destinations.

The first English settlers arrived at Jamestown in 1607 intending to establish a permanent colony from which they could launch attacks on Spanish shipping, search for gold and silver, and produce goods to send back to England. Their charter required them to establish a colony far enough upriver to be safe from Spanish predation, on a spot surrounded on three sides by water, with a landing accessible by deep-draft English ships, and uninhabited by Native Americans. The location chosen for Jamestown turned out to be swampy, mosquito infested, and lacking an adequate supply of fresh water. The colonists also had the misfortune of arriving in the midst of the worst drought in 770 years. The first settlers had no experience living in the wild and required help from the Indians to survive, and in the first year 106 of the original 144 colonists died. Only 60 of 500 colonists who arrived during the "starving time" of 1609–1610 survived. But in 1612 John Rolfe, a survivor from a shipwrecked resupply ship, planted a new type of tobacco that helped rescue the profitability of the colony and drew more settlers. Unfortunately, colonists' hunger for land on which to plant tobacco brought conflict with local Native peoples.

In 1620, 121 Separatist Puritan men, women, and children (often called Pilgrims) set sail from England on the Mayflower, bound for North America. Led by William Bradford (1647–1648), who would later publish his recollections of the founding and settlement in *Of Plymouth Plantation*, they hoped to establish a religious colony free from the persecution they had suffered in England. Their charter directed them to land in the northern part of Virginia now known as New York/New Jersey, but after encountering storms and running low on supplies, they landed far to the north, at Plymouth Rock, MA. Their November arrival was too late to plant crops, and after a freezing, hungry winter, fewer than half the original colonists remained. The local Wampanoag Indians, led by Squanto and Massasoit, taught the Pilgrims how to plant corn, squash, and beans, as well as which plants and animals were safe to eat. This initial cooperation, essential to the Pilgrims' survival, eventually gave way to conflict as Europeans continued to encroach upon Indian lands.

In 1681 William Penn founded a settlement in Pennsylvania. Intending it as a religious haven for persecuted Quakers, Penn also wanted the colony to maintain friendly relations with Native Americans. Because of its relatively late settlement, Europeans in Pennsylvania did not experience the same hardships as colonists in Chesapeake or New England. In 1682 Penn and the first group of Quakers arrived and immediately negotiated to purchase land in the Pennsylvania colony from the Leni Lenape. The religious and cultural tolerance that were written into the charter and the 1683 Frame of Government attracted settlers from across the United Kingdom, Germany, and Holland. Once in the colonies, all of the settlers had to remain loyal to the British Crown and the colony in which they resided and to work to establish permanent settlements.

STANDARDS ADDRESSED

NCHS U.S. History Content Standards, Grades 5–12:

- Why the Americas attracted Europeans, why they brought enslaved Africans to their colonies, and how Europeans struggled for control of North America and the Caribbean
- How political, religious, and social institutions emerged in the English colonies
- How the values and institutions of European economic life took root in the colonies and how slavery reshaped European and African life in the Americas

CCSS for Literacy in History/Social Studies, Grade 6–8:

- Determine the central ideas or information of a primary or secondary source; provide an accurate summary of the source distinct from prior knowledge or opinions.
- Cite specific textual evidence to support analysis of primary and secondary sources.

LESSON 1

ORGANIZING QUESTION

Why was living in the Jamestown colony so difficult?

STRATEGIES USED

Annotation, Think Write Pair Share

MATERIALS NEEDED

1. Locate the following online sources to show to the class:
   - ✓ Map: John Smith's (1612) *A Map of Virginia: With a Description of the Country, the Commodities, People, Government and Religion*, available at http://www.virtualjamestown.org/jsmap_large.html
   - ✓ Drawing: Historic Jamestown's (n.d.a) *Growth of Jamestown*, available at http://apva.org/rediscovery/page.php?page_id=193

2. One copy per student of these primary sources:
   - ✓ List of Settlers: Historic Jamestown's (n.d.b) *Original Settlers and Occupations*, available at http://apva.org/rediscovery/page.php?page_id=31
   - ✓ First-Person Account: "Winter 1609–1610: The Starving Time" section from George Percy's (1624) *A True Relation of the Proceedings and Occurances* [sic] *of Moment which have happened in Virginia . . .*, available at http://nationalhumanitiescenter.org/pds/amerbegin/settlement/text2/JamestownPercyRelation.pdf
   - ✓ Laws: Excerpts from *Lawes Divine, Morall, and Martiall* (1610–1611; simplified version), available at http://www.historyisfun.org/pdf/Laws-at-Jamestown/Lawes_Divine_Morall_and_Martiall.pdf

3. Post-it notes

LESSON PLAN

Lesson Hook: Display John Smith's (1612) map on a screen as students enter the room. As class begins, have students answer the following questions on a Post-it note:

- What details do you notice from the map about land, resources, and people?

- What is your hypothesis about the location and time period of the map?

After a few minutes, have students share their observations and hypotheses about the location and time period from the questions. Clarify that this is John Smith's map of Virginia made in 1612.

Using only the map as a clue, have them predict what might be some potential incentives and challenges to settling in this area in the 1600s. List their responses on the board, which then serve as a reminder throughout the lesson.

The Organizing Question: Explain that students will look at a variety of primary sources about the Jamestown experience to answer the organizing question: Why was living in the Jamestown colony so difficult?

Examine the Sources: *Annotation*—Give students a copy of Historic Jamestown's (n.d.b) *Original Settlers and Occupations*. As they read the document, have them annotate (i.e., make notes of their thinking in the margins) unusual things they notice, what jobs were represented, who or what might have been missing, and questions they have. Discuss these annotations with students and have them predict what might be some potential challenges or problems for the Jamestown settlers, based only on this document. Show Historic Jamestown's (n.d.a) *Growth of Jamestown* illustration and explain the fort and fortifications built there.

Think Write Pair Share—Tell students that their search for clues will continue as they examine more primary sources to answer the organizing question. Give half of the class a copy of "Winter 1609–1610: The Starving Time" (Percy, 1624) and give the other half of the class excerpts from *Lawes Divine, Morall, and Martiall* (1610–1611). Have students read individually and annotate the document for important facts, questions, and clues to help predict what life was like in the Jamestown colony.

Make a Hypothesis: Next, have students find a partner with a different document. Partners should share their annotations, summarize their document, and answer these questions:
- Based on your two documents, what do you think were some challenges for the settlers that made Jamestown such a hard place to live?
- What evidence from the documents leads you to that conclusion?
- How did the primary sources portray events in a different way than the textbook?

End class by having students share their responses with the whole group or have students write their responses as an assessment for the lesson.

LESSON 2

ORGANIZING QUESTION

How did conflict and compromise shape life in New England?

STRATEGIES USED

Concept Map, Modified Jigsaw

MATERIALS NEEDED

1. Book: William Bradford's (1630–1647/1908) "Of Plymouth Plantation, Book Two," available at http://mith.umd.edu/eada/html/display.php?docs=bradford_history.xml. Make four or five copies of these sections, depending on numbers in expert groups:
    ✓ Mayflower Compact (sections 130–133)
    ✓ The Winter (sections 134–135)
    ✓ Native Americans (sections 136–143)
    ✓ Native Americans/Illness (sections 153–154)
    ✓ Harvest (sections 161–162)

2. Two differently colored pencils or highlighters per student
3. One piece of chart paper or poster board per group
4. One copy of the Conflict or Compromise Concept Map (**Handout 3.1**) for each student

LESSON PLAN

Lesson Hook: *Concept Map*—Create two sample concept maps on the board with the words "conflict" and "compromise" in the middle circles. The four outer circles should have these headings: Define It, Draw a Picture, Examples From Your Life, and Examples From History. Let students choose either conflict or compromise and work with a partner to complete the Conflict or Compromise Concept Map (**Handout 3.1**) in their notebooks. Discuss their concept map details and have them show their drawings.

The Organizing Question: Explain that students will examine a primary source for answers to the organizing question: How did conflict and compromise shape life in New England?

Examine the Sources: Explain background information on the Pilgrims, the purpose of the Plymouth colony, and William Bradford's (1647–1648) "Of Plymouth Plantation, Book Two."

Modified Jigsaw—Divide the class into five expert groups, assign each group a section from "Of Plymouth Plantation," and explain how the modified jigsaw activity will work.

- Expert groups: Tell students that they will become experts on a certain section of Bradford's work. Give each student two colored pencils or highlighters and a copy of his or her assigned section. While reading the source in their expert groups, have them highlight or underline examples of conflicts with one color and examples of compromise with another color and discuss the evidence within their expert groups. Remind them that they will teach their information to home groups.

- Home groups: Create mixed groups with at least one person from each expert group represented. Each "expert" should give a summary of his or her section and explain evidence of conflict and/or compromise from the text. When all experts are finished, the home groups will have a variety of clues or evidence to answer the question.

Make the Hypothesis: On chart paper or poster board, have each home group create a visual that uses evidence from the text to answer the organizing question. As groups present their work, highlight similarities and differences in their interpretations of conflict and compromise. Review their graphic organizers from the lesson hook. Have students add information or revise their concept maps based on information learned about Plymouth.

HANDOUT 3.1
CONFLICT OR COMPROMISE CONCEPT MAP

Define It

Draw a Picture

Conflict or Compromise

Examples From
Your Life

Examples
From History

LESSON 3

ORGANIZING QUESTION

How did three different colonies in British North America lay the foundation for representative government?

STRATEGIES USED

Mind Map; Give One, Get One; Reciprocal Reading

MATERIALS NEEDED

1. One copy per student of Three Government Documents (**Handout 3.2**), which contains:
   - ✓ The Great Law: Pennsylvania Charter (1680/1976; *Note:* Students will need help with the sentence structure, lack of punctuation, and vocabulary in this source. You may want to model this source as a whole-class example and use the other two in the reciprocal reading strategy.)
   - ✓ Mayflower Compact, 1620
   - ✓ An Ordinance and Constitution for Council and Assembly in Virginia (1621)

2. One copy per student of the Representative Government Graphic Organizer (**Handout 3.3**)
3. Blank white paper and markers or colored pencils for every student

LESSON PLAN

Lesson Hook: *Mind Map*—As students enter the classroom, have a sample mind map drawn on the board with the words "representative government" in the middle circle. Give students blank white paper and colored pencils or markers and have them create their own mind map by brainstorming what that concept means to them.

The Organizing Question: Explain that students will examine three primary sources to develop a hypothesis for the organizing question: How did three different colonies in British North America lay the foundation of representative government?

35

Examine the Sources: *Give One, Get One*—Have students take their mind map from the lesson hook section and find a partner. Set a timer for one minute, and each student should "give" one idea from their mind map and "get" one idea from their partner. Allow students to switch partners three or four times. Have students share their responses and chart them on the board as you guide the class to develop an accurate definition with examples of representative government. Encourage students to add ideas to their own mind map as you chart them on the board. Give students a copy of Three Government Documents (**Handout 3.2**) and the Representative Government Graphic Organizer (**Handout 3.3**). Direct students' attention to the date of the documents and briefly review what was happening in the 1600s in British North America.

Reciprocal Reading—Divide the class into groups of four and assign each group one of the three documents in **Handout 3.2** to carefully read and examine. Within their groups, they should divide into these reciprocal reading roles:

- Reader: Read the passage out loud, stopping every two or three sentences.
- Main Idea Master: For each two- to three-sentence passage, help your group figure out the main idea from that section.
- Vocabulary Locator: Locate difficult vocabulary words and try to use context clues to help determine their meaning.
- Clarifier and Clue Finder: At the end of each passage, help your group clarify the meaning of the sentences and decide if that section provides any clues to answer the organizing question.

As students read the documents, remind them to stop every two to three sentences, to discuss that section using their chosen roles, and to complete **Handout 3.3** for their document.

Make a Hypothesis: Once groups are finished with their specific source, have each group share the source and what they wrote in the main idea, vocabulary, and clues sections of **Handout 3.3**. All students should complete the handout as groups present their work. Guide the students to answer the similarities and differences question on the handout as a whole class. Remind students of their mind map from the lesson hook that defines the concept of representative government.

Using that concept definition, have students work in their groups to create a hypothesis on **Handout 3.3** that answers the organizing question. Require them to use evidence from all three documents for support. Allow them to share hypotheses and discuss which ideas from the lesson hook were reflected in the three foundational documents.

HANDOUT 3.2
THREE GOVERNMENT DOCUMENTS

Although colonists may not have known it at the time, each of these documents lays the foundation for representative government in the British Colonies. Enacted for Pennsylvania, New England, and Virginia, the laws outline different qualifications for participation in government while at the same time opening the door to the possibility of greater inclusiveness.

THE GREAT LAW, 1682

Chapter 67: And to the End that it may be known who those are that in this Province and territories thereunto belonging have Right of freemen to Choose or to be Chosen and with the Proprietary and Governor make and Enact Laws that Every Inhabitant of the said Province and Territories thereunto Annexed that is or Shall be a purchase of one hundred Acres of Land and hath seated the Same his Heirs and Assigns and Every person who Shall have paid his passage and taken up his fifty Acres of Land and Seated the Same and every inhabitant Artificer or Other Resident in the Said Province that payeth Scott and Lott to the Government Shall be Deemed and accounted A freeman of this Province and territory thereof and Such only Shall have Rights of Election or being Elected to any Service in the Government thereof provided also and be it further Enacted by the Authority aforesaid that all Persons holding any office in this Province or the Territory thereunto belonging or that hath or shall have Right to Choose or to be Chosen Members in Assembly Shall be Such as shall first Subscribe this following declaration: I do hereby freely acknowledge and Solemnly declare and Promise fidelity and Lawful obedience to William Penn Son & Heir of Sir William Penn deceased and his Heirs and Assigns as Rightful Proprietary and Governor of the Same according to the Kings Letters Patents and Deeds of Grant and easement from James Duke of York and Albany &c. and that I will never Act nor do by Word or Deed Directly nor Indirectly any thing nor Consent to nor Conceal any Person or thing whatsoever to the breach of this Solemn Engagement in Witness of Which I have hereunto Set my hand this day of in the year . . .

Chapter 68: And that Elections may not be Corruptly managed upon which the present and future good of the province so much depends be it Enacted by the Authority aforesaid that all Elections of Members as Representatives of the People and freemen of the Province of Pennsylvania and Territories Annexed to Serve in the Assembly there of shall be free and Voluntary and that the Elector that shall Receive any reward or Gift in meat drink monies or Otherwise shall forfeit his Right to Elect and Such Person as Shall give promise or Bestow any Such Reward as aforesaid to be elected shall forfeit his Election and be thereby Incapable to Serve as aforesaid and the Assembly Shall be Sole Judges of the Regularity or Irregularity of the Elections of the Members thereof.

HANDOUT 3.2, CONTINUED

THE MAYFLOWER COMPACT, 1620

IN THE NAME OF GOD, AMEN. We, whose names are underwritten, the Loyal Subjects of our dread Sovereign Lord King *James*, by the Grace of God, of *Great Britain, France,* and *Ireland*, King, *Defender of the Faith*, &c. Having undertaken for the Glory of God, and Advancement of the Christian Faith, and the Honour of our King and Country, a Voyage to plant the first Colony in the northern Parts of *Virginia*; Do by these Presents, solemnly and mutually, in the Presence of God and one another, covenant and combine ourselves together into a civil Body Politick, for our better Ordering and Preservation, and Furtherance of the Ends aforesaid: And by Virtue hereof do enact, constitute, and frame, such just and equal Laws, Ordinances, Acts, Constitutions, and Officers, from time to time, as shall be thought most meet and convenient for the general Good of the Colony; unto which we promise all due Submission and Obedience. **IN WITNESS** whereof we have hereunto subscribed our names at *Cape-Cod* the eleventh of November, in the Reign of our Sovereign Lord King *James*, of *England, France,* and *Ireland*, the eighteenth, and of *Scotland* the fifty-fourth, *Anno Domini*; 1620.
[signed]

AN ORDINANCE AND CONSTITUTION FOR COUNCIL AND ASSEMBLY IN VIRGINIA, JULY 24, 1621

We therefore . . . do hereby order and declare that from henceforward there be two supreme Councils in Virginia . . . the one of which Councils to be called the Council of State and whose office shall chiefly be assisting with the care, advice, and circumspection to the . . . Governor. [They] shall be chosen, nominated, placed, and displaced from time to time by us, the said Treasurer, Council, and Company and our successors. [The] Council of State shall consist for the present only of those person whose names are here inserted . . . And this Council is to be always, or for the most part, residing about or near the . . . Governor. The other Council, more generally, to be called by the Governor . . . yearly . . . and not oftener but for very extraordinary and important occasions, shall consist for present of the said Council of State and of two Burgesses out of every town, hundred, and other particular plantation to be . . . chosen by the inhabitants. [It] shall be called the General Assembly [and] all matters shall be decided, determined, and ordered by the greater part of the voices then present, reserving always to the Governor a [veto]. And this General Assembly shall have free power to treat, consult, and conclude [and also] to make, ordain, and enact such general laws and orders for the behalf of the of the said Colony and the good government thereof as shall [from] time to time be appear necessary.

HANDOUT 3.3
REPRESENTATIVE GOVERNMENT GRAPHIC ORGANIZER

Primary source	Main ideas from this source	Challenging vocabulary words (What context clues might help define them?)	How does this source help answer the organizing question?
Pennsylvania Charter, 1680			
Mayflower Compact, 1620			
An Ordinance and Constitution for Council and Assembly in Virginia, 1621			

1. How did these three different colonies in British North America lay the foundation of representative government? _____

_____

_____

_____

2. What similarities and/or differences did you notice in these documents? _____

_____

_____

_____

3. My hypothesis is: _____

_____

_____

_____

1650-1750

CHAPTER 4

COLONIAL DEVELOPMENT

... of America, where People do not enquire concerning a Stranger, What is he? but, What can he do? If he has any useful Art, he is welcome; and if he exercises it and behaves well, he will be respected by all that know him; but a mere Man of Quality, who on that Account wants to live upon the Public, by some Office or Salary, will be despis'd and disregarded ... –Benjamin Franklin, Information to those who would Remove to America, 1782

HISTORICAL BACKGROUND: WHAT DO I NEED TO KNOW?

New arrivals to America continued to die at alarming rates until the early 18th century, but by the middle of the 17th century, the American colonies had become more stable. Regular trade brought supplies, farmers began to grow more of their own food, and ties to English and European markets brought greater profit across the British colonies. The economies of New England and the Middle Colonies produced diverse commodities based on natural resources that brought moderate but stable profitability to a wide variety of people.

Word of the opportunities available in the British colonies resonated with Europeans suffering from economic and political instability and ongoing wars.

Land ownership rates in England, where some 10% of people owned around 90% of the land, resulted in migrations to the cities in the 16th, 17th, and 18th centuries. In British America, by contrast, a high ratio of land ownership to population saw around 90% of White families owning land. In all of the colonies, property ownership brought the right of political participation unheard of in England.

Companies dedicated to encouraging colonization wrote pamphlets and brochures to advertise these opportunities. For Europeans who could not read, maps of the Americas usually contained elaborate depictions (called *cartouches*) of the mapmaker's vision of life in the colonies.

The labor-intensive, but immensely profitable, plantation economies of Chesapeake, the Carolinas, and Georgia lured an ever-increasing number of settlers. Europeans generally arrived as indentured servants and gained their freedom after working for 5 to 7 years to repay the costs of their passage. The involuntary migration of Africans brought a more permanent labor force. Although African nations captured and sold slaves to Europeans on the coast, the transatlantic African slave trade originated with Portuguese traders. Many Africans died on the brutal Middle Passage across the Atlantic, but enough survived to ensure profitability.

In reaction to the uncertainty of indentured servitude, White planters slowly institutionalized slavery in the American colonies, first defining slavery as a lifetime condition in the 1650s. In the 1660s, Virginia mandated that a child followed the condition of the mother, ensuring that children born to slaves would remain slaves. By the end of the decade, the British colonies had passed laws to equate slavery with being Black and removed prohibitions against enslaving Christians.

Maturing colonies were not necessarily stable colonies. A series of rebellions in the 1670s and 1680s revealed a deep dissatisfaction with elite control over resources and opportunity, particularly regarding access to land and the political opportunity that came with it. By the 1730s colonists also felt that although the colonies prospered, the spiritual side of colonial life was lacking. Into the lives of an increasingly formalized Protestant church structure came the Great Awakening. Although drawing thousands of Americans from all stations in life toward a more evangelical life, the movement also had the effect of splitting many denominations and congregations into enthusiastic supporters, called "New Lights," and more conservative "Old Lights," who frowned on the revivalists' preaching style, message, and meetings. As colonies began to accept different denominations into their borders, it brought Americans closer to the idea that no single church, denomination, or religion ought to have the support of the government.

STANDARDS ADDRESSED

NCHS U.S. History Content Standards, Grades 5–12:
- How political, religious, and social institutions emerged in the English colonies
- How the values and institutions of European economic life took root in the colonies, and how slavery reshaped European and African life in America

CCSS for Literacy in History/Social Studies, Grade 6–8:
- Determine the central ideas or information of a primary or secondary source; provide an accurate summary of the source distinct from prior knowledge or opinions.
- Cite specific textual evidence to support analysis of primary and secondary sources.
- Integrate visual information (e.g., in charts, graphs, photographs, videos, or maps) with other information in print and digital texts.

LESSON 1

ORGANIZING QUESTION

How were maps used to attract settlers to North America?

STRATEGIES USED

Think Aloud, Map Analysis

MATERIALS NEEDED

1. A laptop or iPad for every three students (*Note:* You may choose to print the online maps listed below and give students paper copies. If technology resources are available, the online versions allow you to zoom in on map details.)

2. Online maps:
   ✓ Nicholas Visscher's (1690) *Novi Belgii Novæque Angliæ: nec non partis Virginiæ tabula multis in locis emendata*, available at http://www.loc.gov/item/97683561/
   ✓ Johann Baptist Homann's (1759) *Virginia, Marylandia et Carolina in America septentrionali Britannorum*, available at http://www.loc.gov/item/73691852/
   ✓ John Smith's (1612) *A Map of Virginia: With a Description of the Country, the Commodities, People, Government and Religion*, available at http://www.virtualjamestown.org/jsmap_large.html

3. One copy per student of the Library of Congress Analyzing Maps template, available at http://www.loc.gov/teachers/usingprimarysources/resources/Analyzing_Maps.pdf

4. One piece of white paper per student

LESSON PLAN

(**Note:** This lesson plan incorporates the John Smith map from Chapter 3, but the lesson has a different organizing question. You may choose to use the map again or substitute it with any online colonial map.)

Lesson Hook: Give students a piece of white paper as they enter the classroom. Begin by asking students to describe how they get directions or find where they need to go on a trip. Most will say Google Maps or a variety of map apps on their phones. Ask students if they know what a cartographer is. Explain the following task to the students and give them 10 minutes to complete it:

> You be the cartographer! Your assignment is to draw a detailed map of the classroom using the blank piece of paper. Use the entire space on the paper and put in objects located throughout the classroom. As you draw your desk, place a star over it.

Once students finish the task, have them trade maps with a partner and briefly determine if they can understand or could follow their partner's map to the starred desk. Then ask them these questions: What was difficult about this task? Does your map accurately represent the objects in the classroom? Where do you see spatial errors in your map?

The Organizing Question: Explain that students will analyze three maps to determine clues to the following question: How were maps used to attract settlers to North America?

Examine the Sources: Begin this section of the lesson by asking students to discuss some reasons cartographers might have been important during the 16th and 17th centuries. Review the features found on most maps (e.g., title, key, scale, etc.) and the meaning of *cartouche* before you begin the map analysis.

Think Aloud—Give students a copy of the Library of Congress Analyzing Maps template. Display an online version of any modern map of the United States, your state, or city. Practice analyzing a map using the Analyzing Maps template. Do a Think Aloud with students and describe what details you notice in the map. Use questions from the Observe, Reflect, and Question sections of the template. End your map analysis by asking students what they learned about the specific place from the map details.

Analyzing Maps—Divide students into groups of two or three with a laptop or iPad in each group. Assign them one of the three maps: Visscher (1690), Homann (1759), or Smith (1612). Ask students to use the questions in the Observe, Reflect, and Question sections of the Analyzing Maps template to prompt their analysis of the map. Have students zoom in on the *cartouche* and try to figure out the images there. Challenge students to think about what the cartographer was trying to depict about the Americas. Allow each of the groups to share its findings on all three maps.

Make a Hypothesis: As student groups share their discoveries about each of the three maps, have the rest of the class write down similarities and differ-

INQUIRY-BASED LESSONS IN U.S. HISTORY

ences in the maps and what they think the cartographer was trying to show about North America. Display the online maps on a screen while students give their explanations. End the lesson by having students work with their group to develop a hypothesis with supporting evidence that answers the organizing question. This could be used as an exit slip for the lesson or could be shared in a whole-group discussion.

LESSON 2

ORGANIZING QUESTION

How did slaves experience the Middle Passage?

STRATEGIES USED

Freewriting, Gallery Walk, Partner Read, Annotating Text

MATERIALS NEEDED

1. One copy of each of these images, posted on the wall or in stations around the room with a piece of chart paper beside each image:
    ✓ Image: *Shipping Slaves Through the Surf, West African Coast. A Cruiser Signalled in Sight* (n.d.), available at http://hitchcock.itc.virginia.edu/SlaveTrade/collection/large/CMI-surf.JPG
    ✓ Image: Pretexat Oursel's (n.d.) *Top Deck of French Slave Ship*, available at http://hitchcock.itc.virginia.edu/SlaveTrade/collection/large/E009.JPG
    ✓ Image: Richard Drake's (1860) *Scene in the Hold of the "Blood-Stained Gloria" (Middle Passage)*, available at http://hitchcock.itc.virginia.edu/SlaveTrade/collection/large/E017.JPG
    ✓ Painting: Francis Meynell's (1845) *Hold of Brazilian Slave Ship*, available at http://hitchcock.itc.virginia.edu/SlaveTrade/collection/large/E029.JPG
    ✓ Image: *Group of Slaves on Parade, Fort Augusta* (1857), available at http://hitchcock.itc.virginia.edu/SlaveTrade/collection/large/iln595d.JPG
    ✓ Sketch: *Stowage of the British Slave Ship Brookes Under the Regulated Slave Trade* (1790), available at http://hitchcock.itc.virginia.edu/SlaveTrade/collection/large/E014.JPG

2. Copies of the following sources for half the class:
    ✓ First-Person Account: Excerpts From Olaudah Equiano's (1789) *The Interesting Narrative of the Life of Olaudah Equiano, Or Gustavus Vassa, The African Written By Himself* (**Handout 4.1**)
    ✓ First-Person Account: Excerpts From Alexander Falconbridge's (1792) *An Account of the Slave Trade from the Coast of Africa* (**Handout 4.2**)

3. Chart paper and markers
4. Highlighters for each student

LESSON PLAN

Lesson Hook: *Freewriting*—Because this lesson contains difficult content for students, allow them a few minutes to freewrite in their notes about what they remember about slavery from previous classes and what questions they wonder about based on their background knowledge. You may also want to show any online image of slavery or the slave trade in the United States to prompt their thinking about the topic.

The Organizing Question: Explain that students will examine several images and read two first-person accounts for clues to answer the organizing question: How did slaves experience the Middle Passage?

Examine the Sources: *Gallery Walk*—Begin this part of the lesson by explaining the Middle Passage and showing the routes on a map. Tell students that they will participate in a Gallery Walk and examine images to predict some details about what life was like for slaves during the Middle Passage. Have students choose a partner and give each pair a marker. Assign the pairs to a station to start the Gallery Walk. Their task is to examine the image first, then write on the chart paper what they notice and what they think it tells them about the Middle Passage. Have the students rotate clockwise, adding their comments and responding to others' written ideas. When they have returned to the image where they started, have them read all of the responses and report to the class what they think the image tells them. As a class, make a list of what questions they have about the images in the Gallery Walk.

Partner Read/Annotating Text—Explain to students that they will now examine two first-person accounts of the Middle Passage from a slave and a doctor. Divide the class in half and give one half **Handout 4.1** and the other half **Handout 4.2**. Allow students to partner with someone who has the same text. As they are reading, have them look for answers to the questions charted on the board and the lesson's organizing question. As they find clues to any of these questions, have them highlight them in the text. Encourage them to read one section at a time, stop and discuss it, and write main ideas or questions they have in the margins beside that section. As partner groups finish reading and analyzing their text, have them find two people who read the other text and form a group of four. Their task is to explain their sources and to share the main ideas and clues they located.

Make a Hypothesis: After students share both texts, have them work as groups to create a hypothesis that answers the organizing question. Require them to use both first-person accounts and the images in the Gallery Walk as evidence to support their hypotheses. Allow groups to share hypotheses with the class and evaluate how well other groups use evidence as support.

HANDOUT 4.1
EXCERPTS FROM OLAUDAH EQUIANO'S (1789) *THE INTERESTING NARRATIVE OF THE LIFE OF OLAUDAH EQUIANO, OR GUSTAVUS VASSA, THE AFRICAN WRITTEN BY HIMSELF*

The first object which saluted my eyes when I arrived on the coast was the sea, and a slave ship, which was then riding at anchor, and waiting for its cargo. These filled me with astonishment, which was soon converted into terror when I was carried on board. I was immediately handled and tossed up to see if I were sound by some of the crew; and I was now persuaded that I had gotten into a world of bad spirits, and that they were going to kill me. Their complexions too differing so much from ours, their long hair, and the language they spoke, (which was very different from any I had ever heard) united to confirm me in this belief. Indeed such were the horrors of my views and fears at the moment, that, if ten thousand worlds had been my own, I would have freely parted with them all to have exchanged my condition with that of the meanest slave in my own country.

When I looked round the ship too and saw a large furnace or copper boiling, and a multitude of black people of every description chained together, every one of their countenances expressing dejection and sorrow, I no longer doubted of my fate; and, quite overpowered with horror and anguish, I fell motionless on the deck and fainted. When I recovered a little I found some black people about me, who I believed were some of those who brought me on board, and had been receiving their pay; they talked to me in order to cheer me, but all in vain. I asked them if we were not to be eaten by those white men with horrible looks, red faces, and loose hair. They told me I was not; and one of the crew brought me a small portion of spirituous liquor in a wine glass; but, being afraid of him, I would not take it out of his hand. One of the blacks therefore took it from him and gave it to me, and I took a little down my palate, which, instead of reviving me, as they thought it would, threw me into the greatest consternation at the strange feeling it produced, having never tasted any such liquor before.

Soon after this the blacks who brought me on board went off, and left me abandoned to despair. I now saw myself deprived of all chance of returning to my native country, or even the least glimpse of hope of gaining the shore, which I now considered as friendly; and I even wished for my former slavery in preference to my present situation, which was filled with horrors of every kind, still heightened by my ignorance of what I was to undergo. I was not long suffered to indulge my grief; I was soon put down under the decks, and there I received such a salutation in my nostrils as I had never experienced in my life: so that, with the loathsomeness of the stench, and crying together, I became so sick and low that I was not able to eat, nor had I the least desire to taste any thing. I now wished for the last friend, death, to relieve me; but soon, to my grief, two of the white men offered me eatables; and, on my refusing to eat, one of them held me fast by the hands, and laid me across I think the windlass, and tied my feet, while the other flogged me severely. I had never experienced any thing of this kind before; and although, not being used to the water, I naturally feared that element the first time I saw it, yet

HANDOUT 4.1, CONTINUED

nevertheless, could I have got over the nettings, I would have jumped over the side, but I could not; and, besides, the crew used to watch us very closely who were not chained down to the decks, lest we should leap into the water: and I have seen some of these poor African prisoners most severely cut for attempting to do so, and hourly whipped for not eating. This indeed was often the case with myself.

In a little time after, amongst the poor chained men, I found some of my own nation, which in a small degree gave ease to my mind. I inquired of these what was to be done with us; they gave me to understand we were to be carried to these white people's country to work for them. I then was a little revived, and thought, if it were no worse than working, my situation was not so desperate: but still I feared I should be put to death, the white people looked and acted, as I thought, in so savage a manner; for I had never seen among any people such instances of brutal cruelty; and this not only shewn towards us blacks, but also to some of the whites themselves. One white man in particular I saw, when we were permitted to be on deck, flogged so unmercifully with a large rope near the foremast, that he died in consequence of it; and they tossed him over the side as they would have done a brute.

This made me fear these people the more; and I expected nothing less than to be treated in the same manner. I could not help expressing my fears and apprehensions to some of my countrymen: I asked them if these people had no country, but lived in this hollow place (the ship): they told me they did not, but came from a distant one. The stench of the hold while we were on the coast was so intolerably loathsome, that it was dangerous to remain there for any time, and some of us had been permitted to stay on the deck for the fresh air; but now that the whole ship's cargo were confined together, it became absolutely pestilential. The closeness of the place, and the heat of the climate, added to the number in the ship, which was so crowded that each had scarcely room to turn himself, almost suffocated us. This produced copious perspirations, so that the air soon became unfit for respiration, from a variety of loathsome smells, and brought on a sickness among the slaves, of which many died, thus falling victims to the improvident avarice, as I may call it, of their purchasers.

This wretched situation was again aggravated by the galling of the chains, now become insupportable; and the filth of the necessary tubs, into which the children often fell, and were almost suffocated. The shrieks of the women, and the groans of the dying, rendered the whole a scene of horror almost inconceivable. One day they had taken a number of fishes; and when they had killed and satisfied themselves with as many as they thought fit, to our astonishment who were on the deck, rather than give any of them to us to eat as we expected, they tossed the remaining fish into the sea again, although we begged and prayed for some as well as we could, but in vain; and some of my countrymen, being pressed by hunger, took an opportunity, when they thought no one saw them, of trying to get a little privately; but they were discovered, and the attempt procured them some very severe floggings.

One day, when we had a smooth sea and moderate wind, two of my wearied countrymen who were chained together (I was near them at the time), preferring death to such a life of misery, somehow made through the nettings and jumped into the sea:

HANDOUT 4.1, CONTINUED

immediately another quite dejected fellow, who, on account of his illness, was suffered to be out of irons, also followed their example; and I believe many more would very soon have done the same if they had not been prevented by the ship's crew, who were instantly alarmed. Those of us that were the most active were in a moment put down under the deck, and there was such a noise and confusion amongst the people of the ship as I never heard before, to stop her, and get the boat out to go after the slaves. However two of the wretches were drowned, but they got the other, and afterwards flogged him unmercifully for thus attempting to prefer death to slavery. In this manner we continued to undergo more hardships than I can now relate, hardships which are inseparable from this accursed trade. Many a time we were near suffocation from the want of fresh air, which we were often without for whole days together. This, and the stench of the necessary tubs, carried off many.

At last we came in sight of the island of Barbadoes, at which the whites on board gave a great shout, and made many signs of joy to us. We did not know what to think of this; but as the vessel drew nearer we plainly saw the harbour, and other ships of different kinds and sizes; and we soon anchored amongst them off Bridge Town. Many merchants and planters now came on board, though it was in the evening. They put us in separate parcels, and examined us attentively. They also made us jump, and pointed to the land, signifying we were to go there. We thought by this we should be eaten by these ugly men, as they appeared to us; and, when soon after we were all put down under the deck again, there was much dread and trembling among us, and nothing but bitter cries to be heard all the night from these apprehensions, insomuch that at last the white people got some old slaves from the land to pacify us. They told us we were not to be eaten, but to work, and were soon to go on land, where we should see many of our country people. This report eased us much; and sure enough, soon after we were landed, there came to us Africans of all languages.

We were conducted immediately to the merchant's yard, where we were all pent up together like so many sheep in a fold, without regard to sex or age. As every object was new to me every thing I saw filled me with surprise. What struck me first was that the houses were built with stories, and in every other respect different from those in Africa: but I was still more astonished on seeing people on horseback. We were not many days in the merchant's custody before we were sold after their usual manner, which is this:— On a signal given,(as the beat of a drum) the buyers rush at once into the yard where the slaves are confined, and make choice of that parcel they like best. The noise and clamour with which this is attended, and the eagerness visible in the countenances of the buyers, serve not a little to increase the apprehensions of the terrified Africans, who may well be supposed to consider them as the ministers of that destruction to which they think themselves devoted. In this manner, without scruple, are relations and friends separated, most of them never to see each other again.

HANDOUT 4.2
EXCERPTS FROM ALEXANDER FALCONBRIDGE'S (1792) *AN ACCOUNT OF THE SLAVE TRADE FROM THE COAST OF AFRICA*

About eight o'clock in the morning the negroes are generally brought upon deck. Their irons being examined, a long chain, which is locked to a ring-bolt, fixed in the deck, is run through the rings of the shackles of the men, and then locked to another ring-bolt, fixed also in the deck. By this means fifty or sixty, and sometimes more, are fastened to one chain, in order to prevent them from rising, or endeavoring to escape. If the weather proves favorable, they are permitted to remain in that situation till four or five in the afternoon, when they are disengaged from the chain, and sent down.

The diet of the negroes, while on board, consists chiefly of horse-beans, boiled to the consistency of a pulp, of boiled yams and rice, and sometimes of a small quantity of beef or pork. The latter are frequently taken from the provisions laid in for the jailers. They sometimes make use of a sauce, composed of palm-oil, mixed with flour, water, and pepper, which the jailers slabber-sauce. Yams are the favorite food of the Ebo, or Bight negroes, and rice or corn, of those from the Gold and Windward Coasts each preferring the produce of their native soil.

They are commonly fed twice a day, about eight o'clock in the morning and four in the afternoon. In most ships they are only fed with their own food once a day. Their food is served up to them in tubs, about the size of a small water bucket. They are placed round these tubs in companies of ten to each tub, out of which they feed themselves with wooden spoons.

Upon the negroes refusing to take sustenance, I have seen coals of fire, glowing hot, put on a shovel, and placed so near their lips, as to scorch and burn them. And this has been accompanied with threats, of forcing them to swallow the coals, if they any longer persisted in refusing to eat. These means have generally had the desired effect. I have also been credibly informed, that a certain captain in the slave trade, poured melted lead on such of the negroes as obstinately refused their food.

The hardships and inconveniencies suffered by the negroes during the passage, are scarcely to be enumerated or conceived. They are far more violently affected by the sea-sickness, than the Europeans. It frequently terminates in death, especially among the women. But the exclusion of the fresh air is among the most intolerable. For the purpose of admitting this needful refreshment, most of the ships in the slave-trade are provided, between the decks, with five or six airports. On each side of the ship, of about six inches in length, and four in breadth in addition to which, some few ships, but not one in twenty, have what they denominate wind-sails. But whenever the sea is rough, and the rain heavy, it becomes necessary to shut these, and every other conveyance by which the air is admitted. The fresh air being thus excluded, the negroes rooms very soon grow intolerably hot. The confined air, rendered noxious by the effluvia exhaled from their bodies, and by being repeatedly breathed, soon produces fevers and fluxes, which generally carries off great numbers of them.

LESSON 3

THE ORGANIZING QUESTION

How did American colonists experience the Great Awakening?

STRATEGIES USED

5W Review (Who? What? When? Where? Why?), Role Play

MATERIALS NEEDED

1. Jon Scieszka's (1989) *The True Story of the Three Little Pigs* (*Note:* If you can't find this children's book, do the lesson hook using the Humpty Dumpty nursery rhyme.)
2. Copies of the following primary source excerpts for members of each of the four groups:
   ✓ Nathan Cole's (ca. 1740/1967) "Spiritual Travels" (**Handout 4.3**)
   ✓ William Shurtleff's (1745/1967) "Letter to Those who Refuse to Admit Whitefield" (**Handout 4.4**)
   ✓ Edward Holyoke's (1744/1967) "The Testimony of Harvard College against George Whitefield" (**Handout 4.5**)
   ✓ Josiah Smith's (1740/1967) "Whitefield's Character and Preaching" (**Handout 4.6**)

LESSON PLAN

Lesson Hook: Begin class by having students write down the "facts" in the story of the Three Little Pigs. Ask them to list the characters, to explain details about the setting, and to describe the sequence of events. Allow several students to share their version of the story. Now read aloud John Scieszka's (1989) *The True Story of the Three Little Pigs* and have students see how well it matches their story. Have students listen for similarities and differences in their story and the book's version. Ask them to think about why the stories might be so different and lead them, if needed, to the concept of multiple perspectives. Have them share examples of multiple perspectives on historical events that they have already learned in class.

The Organizing Question: Explain that students will examine four different primary source accounts to help answer the organizing question: How did American colonists experience the Great Awakening?

Examine the Sources: *5W Review (Who? What? When? Where? Why?)*—Begin class by having students write the 5W Review questions in their notes. With a partner, have them review the Great Awakening by writing down answers to the 5W questions:

- Who was involved?
- What was it?
- When did it happen?
- Where did it take place?
- Why was it important?

Role Play—Divide the class into four sections and assign each section a person: Cole, Shurtleff, Holyoke, and Smith. Give students copies of the primary source written by their assigned person (**Handouts 4.3, 4.4, 4.5,** and **4.6**) and allow them to sit together in four large circles to examine the document together. Explain to them that they are going to role-play a discussion among four people who experienced events or effects of the Great Awakening.

Their first task is to read the handout carefully and underline or highlight clues about that author's background, events he witnessed, and opinions. Have students read one section at a time and discuss it, making notes on their document. Circulate, answer questions, and clarify vocabulary words as needed. Make sure that each group has an accurate understanding of its person and point of view before you organize discussion groups.

Once all students are finished analyzing the documents, reorganize the class into groups of four with all four "people" represented in the discussion circle. Tell the students to role-play their characters, introduce themselves, and explain who they are. Prompt them to begin discussing the Great Awakening from the point of view of what their person experienced, thought, or wrote about. Encourage them to talk about specific examples from their documents.

Make a Hypothesis: As the role-play group finishes the discussion, have them develop a hypothesis that answers the organizing question. Require them to give evidence from each of the four sources. If time permits, students could create a newspaper story about the Great Awakening with headlines, pictures, and "interviews" with the four people in the documents.

HANDOUT 4.3
NATHAN COLE'S (CA. 1740/1967)
"SPIRITUAL TRAVELS"

Now it pleased God to send Mr. Whitefield into this land; and my hearing of his preaching at Philadelphia, like one of the old apostles, and many thousands flocking to hear him preach the Gospel, and the great numbers were converted to Christ, I felt the Spirit of God drawing me by conviction; I longed to see and hear him and wished he would come this way. I heard he was come to New York and the Jerseys and great multitudes flocking after him under great concern for their souls which brought on my concern more and more, hoping soon to see him . . .

Then on a sudden, in the morning about 8 or 9 of the clock there came a messenger and said Mr. Whitefield preached at Hartford and Wethersfield yesterday and is to preach at Middletown this morning at ten of the clock. I was in my field at work. I dropped my tool that I had in my hand and ran home to my wife, telling her to make ready quickly to go and hear Mr. Whitefield preach at Middletown, then ran to my pasture for my horse with all my might, fearing that I should be too late. Having my horse, I with my wife soon mounted the horse and went forward as fast as I thought the horse could bear; and when my horse got much out of breath, I would get down an put my wife on the saddle and bid her ride as fast as she could and not stop or slack for me except I bade her, and so I would run until I was much out of breath and then mount my horse again, and so I did several times to favour my horse. We improved every moment to get along as if we were fleeing for our lives, all the while fearing we should be too late to hear the sermon, for we had twelve miles to ride double in little more than an hour and we went round by the upper housen parish. And when we came within about half a mile or a mile of the road that comes down from Hartford, Wethersfield, and Stepney to Middletown, on high land I saw before me a cloud of fog arising. I first thought it came from the great river, but as I came nearer the road I heard a noise of horses' feet coming down the road, and this cloud was a cloud of dust made by the horses' feet. It arose some rods into the air over the tops of hills and trees; and when I came within about 20 rods of the road, I could see men and horses slipping along in the cloud like shadows, and as I drew nearer it seemed like a steady stream of horses and their riders, scarcely a horse more than his length behind another, all of a lather and foam with sweat, their breath rolling out of their nostrils every jump.

. . . and when we got to Middletown old meeting house, there was a great multitude, it was said to be 3 or 4,000 of people, assembled together. We dismounted and shook off our dust, and the ministers were then coming to the meeting house. I turned and looked towards the Great River and saw the ferry boats running swift backward and forward bringing over loads of people, and the oars rowed nimble and quick. Everything, men, horses, and boats seemed to be struggling for life. The land and banks over the river looked black with people and horses; all along the 12 miles I saw no man at work in his field, but all seemed to be gone. When I saw Mr. Whitefield come upon the scaffold, he looked almost angelical; a young, slim, slender youth, before some thousands of people with a bold undaunted countenance. And my hearing how God was with him everywhere as he came along, it solemnized my mind and put me into a trembling fear before he began to preach; for he looked as if he was clothed with authority from the Great God, and a sweet solemn solemnity sat upon his brow, and my hearing him preach gave me a heart wound. By God's blessing, my old foundation was broken up, and I saw that my righteousness would not save me.

HANDOUT 4.4
WILLIAM SHURTLEFF'S (1745/1967) "LETTER TO THOSE WHO REFUSE TO ADMIT WHITEFIELD"

. . . The Reports that were brought among us of Mr. *Whitefield* and his Ministry; of the Multitude that attended it, and the Manner in which they were wrought upon by it, had excited a Thoughtfulness in a great many, even before his Arrival among us: And when he came, you are sensible what Crowds came to hear him, and how generally they were wrought upon by his Preaching. As it made saving Impressions upon some; so where it failed of this, it raised in a great Number a deep and lasting Concern as to their spiritual and eternal Interests. . . . As *People* long'd more to *hear*; so *Ministers* lov'd more to *preach* than they had used to do, and usually spoke with greater Power. Some of them that were Strangers to true and vital Piety before, became now acquainted with it; and others that were grown in a great Measure dead and formal, were quicken'd, stir'd up, and had new Life put into them . . . *Our Assemblies* were vastly throng'd; and it was rare to see a careless and inattentive Hearer among them all. Their thirsty Souls seem'd greedily to drink down every Word that drop'd from the Preacher's Lips. They heard as for their Lives.

. . . And tho' some soon lost their Convictions, and others that went a great Way, have since apostatiz'd and drawn back; yet upon a strict and fair Inquiry, you will find a great many in one Place and another that are exhibiting all the Evidence that can be expected of an effectual and thorough Chance a great many that having been *sometimes Darkness, but being now Light in the Lord, walk as Children of the Light*; and by their good Conversation are bright and shining Ornaments to their Christian Profession.

Some *Ministers* that were great Friends to the Revival of Religion, thro' an ungovern'd, tho' well meant Zeal, have been carried into unbecoming Extreams; and whilst they have been much admir'd and almost idoliz'd by the People, have been left (and partly it may be for that Reason) to fall into great Indiscretions. And so it has been as to *some others*, and I make no Doubt as to some gracious Persons; they have run into Errors of Judgment, and Errors of Practice. Some have strangely given Way to Spiritual Pride; they have discover'd too much of a censorious Spirit one towards another . . .

. . . In the late Times, amidst all the Disorders that have arose, there has been a deep and serious Concern among great Numbers as to the Salvation of their Souls. Not a few we have good Reason to think have been rescued from the *Powers of Darkness*, and become the Subjects of the Redeemer's Kingdom. Now does not this which has occasion'd so much Joy in heaven, and diffused such a Pleasure thro' the whole angelic Hosts, call for Rejoicing from us here upon Earth, and demand our chearful Praises to the GOD of all Grace? Is not such a State as this preferable to that we were formerly in? when it was a rare Thing for any to be converted from the Error of their Way . . . resting in their Attendance upon Ordinances, and in an external Conformity to the divine Will . . .

. . . the Alteration there has been as to the State of Religion in these Churches, all Things being consider'd be for the better and not for the worse; and if Mr. *Whitefield* has had any Hand in the Change . . . I think he ought to be highly valued and regarded by us: that it becomes us to be very thankful to *him*, but above all give *Glory* to God, that has raised up such an Instrument, and made him the Means of so much Good to us.

HANDOUT 4.5
EDWARD HOLYOKE'S (1744/1967) "THE TESTIMONY OF HARVARD COLLEGE AGAINST GEORGE WHITEFIELD"

In regard of the Danger which we apprehend the People and Churches of this Land are in, on the Account of the Rev. Mr. George Whitefield, we have tho't ourselves oblig'd to bear our Testimony, in this public Manner, against him and his Way of Preaching, as tending very much to the Detriment of Religion . . . And we do therefore hereby declare, That we look upon his going about, in an Itinerant Way, especially as he has so much of an enthusiastic Turn, utterly inconsistent with the Peace and Order, if not the very Being of these Churches of Christ.

First, as to the Man himself, whom we look upon as an Enthusiast, a censorious, uncharitable Person, and a Deluder of the People . . . we mean by an *Enthusiast*, one that acts, either according to Dreams, or some sudden Impulses and Impressions upon his Mind, which he fondly imagines to be from the Spirit of God, perswading and inclining him thereby to such and such Actions, tho' he hath no Proof that such Perswasions or Impressions are from the holy Spirit . . . And in what Condition must that People be, who stand ready to be led by a Man that conducts himself according to his Dreams, or some ridiculous and unaccountable Impulses and Impressions on his Mind? And that this is Mr. *Whitefield*'s Manner, is evident both by his Life, his Journals, and his Sermons . . .

. . . we look upon him a *Deluder of the People* . . . And here we mean more especially as to the Collections of Money, which when here before . . . he almost *extorted* from the People. As the Argument he then used was, *the Support and Education of his dear Lambs at the Orphan-House*, who (he told us, he hop'd) might in Time preach the Gospel to us or our Children; so it is not to be doubted, that the People were greatly encouraged to give him largely of their Substance, supposing they were to be under the immediate Tuition and Instruction of himself, as he then made them to believe . . . and this notwithstanding, he hath scarce seen them for these four Years; and besides hath left the Care of them with a Person, whom these Contributors know nothing of, and we ourselves have Reason to believe is little better than a *Quaker*; so that in this Regard we think the People have been greatly deceiv'd.

Secondly, We have as much Reason to dislike and bear Testimony against the *Manner* of his Preaching; and this in Two respects, both as an *Extempore* and as an *Itinerant* Preacher . . . as to his *extempore* Manner of preaching; this we think by no means proper, for it is impossible that any Man should be able to manage any Argument with that Strength, or any Instruction with that Clearness in an *extempore* Manner, as he may with Study and Meditation.

. . . Now by an *Itinerant* Preacher, we understand One that hath no particular Charge of his own, but goes about from Country to Country, or from Town to Town, in any Country, and stands ready to Preach to any Congregation that shall call him to it . . . it is then in his Power to raise the People to any Degree of Warmth he pleases, whereby they stand ready to receive almost any Doctrine he is pleased to broach; as hath been the Case as to all the Itinerant Preachers who have followed Mr. W's Example, and thrust themselves into Towns and Parishes, to the Destruction of all Peace and Order, whereby they have to the great impoverishment of the Community, taken the People from their Work and Business, to attend their Lectures and Exhortations; always fraught with Enthusiasm, and other pernicious Errors . . .

HANDOUT 4.6
JOSIAH SMITH'S (1740/1967) "WHITEFIELD'S CHARACTER AND PREACHING"

I shall next give you my opinion on the manner of his preaching. And here I need not say, nor can my pen describe his action and gesture, in all their strength and decencies. He is certainly a finished preacher, and a great master of pulpit oratory and elocution, while a noble negligence ran thro' his style. Yes his discourses were very extraordinary when we consider how little they were premeditated, and how many of them he gave us, the little time he was with us—Many, I trust, have felt, and will long feel the impressions of his zeal and fire, the passion and flame of his expressions . . .

He appeared to me, in all his discourses, very deeply affected and impressed in his own heart. How did that burn and boil within him, when he spake of the things he had made, touching the King? How was his tongue like the pen of a ready writer? touching as with a coal from the altar! With what a flow of words, what a ready profusion of language, did he speak to us upon the great concern of our souls? . . . The awe, the silence, the attention, which sat upon the face of so great an audience, was an argument, how he could reign over all their powers. Many thought, *He spoke as never man spoke*, before him. So charmed were the people with his manner of address, that they shut up their shops, forgot their secular business, and laid aside their schemes for the world; and the oftener he preached, the keener edge he seemed to put upon their desires of hearing him again! How awfully, with what thunder and sound did he discharge the artillery of Heaven upon us? And yet, how could he soften and melt even a soldier of Ulysses, with the love and mercy of God!

Now we are none of us ignorant, how far the primitive spirit of Christianity has sunk into a mere form of godliness. Irreligion has been rushing in, even upon the Protestant world like a flood; the dearest and most obvious doctrines of the Bible have fallen into low contempt; the principles and systems of our good and pious fathers have been more and more exploded. And now, behold! God seems to have revived the ancient spirit and doctrines. He is raising up our young men, with zeal and courage to stem the torrent. They have been in *labour more abundant*; they have preached with such fire, assiduity, and success; such a solemn awe have they struck upon their hearers; so unaccountably have they conquered the prejudices of many persons; such deep convictions have their sermons produced; so much have they roused and kindled the zeal of ministers and people; so intrepidly do they push through all opposition, that my soul overflows with joy, and my heart is too full to express my hopes. It looks as if some happy period were opening, to bless the world with another reformation. Some great things seem to be upon the anvil, some big prophecy at the birth: God give it strength to bring forth!

1750-1783

CHAPTER 5

THE PATH TO INDEPENDENCE

The Revolution was effected before the war commenced. The Revolution was in the minds and hearts of the people; a change in their religious sentiments, of their duties and obligations . . . This radical change in the principles, opinions, sentiments, and affections of the people was the real American Revolution.—John Adams, Letter to H. Niles, February 13, 1818

HISTORICAL BACKGROUND: WHAT DO I NEED TO KNOW?

Historians sometimes refer to the early 18th century in the British American colonies as a period of "benign neglect," when the colonies largely governed themselves without interference from England. This changed as a result of the French and Indian War, from 1754–1763, which set in motion a series of events that would lead to the American Revolution.

In the colonies, France and its Native American allies fought against the British and their Native allies. Victory in this worldwide war saddled Great Britain with a crushing national debt, a need to defend the newly acquired territory, and obligations to the Native American tribes who had fought against the French. To stem encroachment onto Native lands and to prevent Native

Americans from assisting Spanish or French attempts to invade the Ohio Valley, George III's Proclamation of 1763 prohibited British settlement west of the Appalachians. British colonists, for whom cheap and easily available land promised a chance for wealth and political participation, reacted with protests.

Defense of the territory required a larger military presence in the colonies. British regular troops arrived in American port cities in the Middle and New England colonies, and they sometimes stayed for long periods before moving out to the frontier. Because of the lack of barracks, British commanders invoked established laws requiring civilians to house troops in their homes before the units moved out to the frontier.

The need to pay for the increased military presence required to defend the colonies, as well as the interest and principal on the national debt, required an increased source of revenue. The British North American colonies had never been a source of profit for the government, always costing more to maintain than they generated in tax revenue. At the same time, the era of benign neglect left the colonies as the most lightly taxed, lightly regulated people in the Empire. Beginning in the 1760s, England set out to correct this by making the colonies pay for what Parliament regarded as the colonists' fair share of the financial burden.

In reality, the taxes generated by the various acts passed by Parliament in the 1760s and 1770s would have paid for only a fraction of the increased defense costs, but a firestorm erupted nonetheless. The Stamp Act, which required colonists to affix a government stamp to most documents, brought about widespread protests, while a series of laws meant to both pacify the colonists and assert Parliamentary control reminded Americans of their status as subjects. Colonists protested by burning effigies, tarring and feathering opponents, and engaging in both peaceful and violent petitions and protests. They also used political cartoons to lampoon British officials and criticize colonial policies.

The unrest in the 1770s became focused on the system of government—first with Parliament and eventually with the king himself. In this context many colonists began to question the right of England to govern the colonies. The appearance of Thomas Paine's (1776) *Common Sense* was a milestone in the debates over governance. The pamphlet laid out arguments against the British Crown and in favor of self-governance in language easily understood by common people generally thought incapable of governing themselves.

Even after the outbreak of rebellion and war in 1775, many colonists opposed independence, hoping to reconcile with the mother country. On July 4, 1776, the Continental Congress adopted a Declaration of Independence that listed a series of grievances against the king and made the case for world recognition of the United States of America.

STANDARDS ADDRESSED

NCHS U.S. History Content Standards, Grades 5–12:

- The causes of the American Revolution, the ideas and interests involved in forging the revolutionary movement, and the reasons for the American victory
- The impact of the American Revolution on politics, economy, and society

CCSS for Literacy in History/Social Studies, Grade 6–8:

- Describe how a text presents information (e.g., sequentially, comparatively, causally).
- Determine the central ideas or information of a primary or secondary source; provide an accurate summary of the source distinct from prior knowledge or opinions.
- Cite specific textual evidence to support analysis of primary and secondary sources.

LESSON 1

ORGANIZING QUESTION

How did 18th-century political cartoons reflect tensions between colonists and Great Britain?

STRATEGIES USED

Think Aloud, Analyzing Political Cartoons, Modified Jigsaw

MATERIALS NEEDED

1. One copy per student of the Library of Congress's Analyzing Political Cartoons Guide, available at http://www.loc.gov/teachers/usingprimary sources/resources/Analyzing_Political_Cartoons.pdf

2. An online version of the following source to display for students as a model Think Aloud:
   ✓ Political cartoon: "The repeal, or the funeral of Miss Ame=Stamp" (n.d.), available at http://www.loc.gov/pictures/resource/ppmsca. 15709/

3. Four or five copies of each source per expert group:
   ✓ Political cartoon: Sayer and Bennett's (1774) "The Bostonians Paying the Excise Man, or Tarring and Feathering," available at http://www. loc.gov/pictures/resource/cph.3a11950/
   ✓ Engraving: Paul Revere's (1770) "The Bloody Massacre Perpetrated in King Street Boston on March 5th, 1770 by a Party of the 29th Regt.," available at http://www.loc.gov/pictures/resource/ppmsca.01657/
   ✓ Political cartoon: "The Able Doctor, or, America Swallowing the Bitter Draught" (1774), available at http://www.loc.gov/resource/cph.3g05289/
   ✓ Political cartoon: "A New Method of Macarony Making, as Practised at Boston" (1774), available at http://www.loc.gov/pictures/resource/cph.3a45583/
   ✓ Political cartoon: Elkanah Tisdale's (1795) "The Tory's Day of Judgment," available at http://www.loc.gov/pictures/resource/cph.3a10349/

4. One piece of white copy paper and markers for each student

LESSON PLAN

Lesson Hook: Ask students to brainstorm a list of current student issues or concerns in their school or community. Once they have made a list, have them choose one issue about which they have a strong opinion. Give students blank paper and markers and tell them they have 10 minutes to take a position on this issue and illustrate their position in a visual. Have students share their visuals and discuss similarities and differences in the way students represented their points of view on school or community issues.

The Organizing Question: Explain that students will examine 18th-century political cartoons to determine the answer to the organizing question: How did 18th-century political cartoons reflect tensions between colonists and Great Britain?

Examine the Sources: *Think Aloud* and *Analyzing Political Cartoons*—Display "The repeal, or the funeral of Miss Ame=Stamp" (n.d.) on a screen and give students a copy of the Library of Congress's Analyzing Political Cartoons guide. As a whole class, guide students to respond to the questions in the Observe, Reflect, and Question sections of the guide. Make sure to focus on the cartoonist's opinions on the Stamp Act and what methods he used to persuade the audience.

Modified Jigsaw—Now explain to students that they will examine other political cartoons from the 18th century using the same analysis guide.

Expert groups: Divide the class into five expert groups and give each group copies of one of the political cartoons listed in the Materials Needed section. Explain that students will become experts on their cartoon. As an expert group, they should answer the questions from the Analyzing Political Cartoons guide about their specific cartoon. Remind students to look at words and symbols to help determine each cartoonist's point of view on colonial issues and tensions. Because period political cartoons are often difficult to understand, be ready to provide either copies of the text explanation or website links for students to read about the cartoon if needed.

Home groups: Once students are finished completing the analysis in their expert groups, assign each student in every group a letter such as A, B, C, and so forth. Ask them to join similar letters from other expert groups to create a home group. Once students rearrange into home groups, there should be an expert on each political cartoon. Each expert should share the cartoon, explain the meaning, and analyze the author's purpose for other members of the home group.

Make a Hypothesis: When all students are finished with the cartoon explanations, have the home groups use all five cartoons to make a hypothesis that answers the organizing question. Have one student in each home group write the group's hypothesis and supporting evidence on a paper to turn in with all group members' names included. Allow each group to share its hypothesis with evidence. Discuss the similarities and differences in their hypotheses and relate the techniques used in 18th-century cartoons to those they used in the lesson hook cartoons about current issues.

LESSON 2

ORGANIZING QUESTION

What are the main points in Thomas Paine's (1776) *Common Sense*?

STRATEGIES USED

Think Aloud, Very Important Points (VIPs), Sketching Through the Text

MATERIALS NEEDED

1. One copy per student of Excerpts From Thomas Paine's (1776) *Common Sense* (**Handout 5.1**)
2. One piece of chart paper or poster board and markers for each group of six

LESSON PLAN

Lesson Hook: Ask students to write down answers to the following questions:

*   What does it mean when a person has common sense?
*   Have you ever heard anyone use this concept? If so, what or who were they describing?

Have students share their responses and personal stories.

The Organizing Question: Explain that students will read and analyze excerpts of a book written in 1776 and answer this organizing question: What are the main points in Thomas Paine's *Common Sense*?

Examine the Sources: *Think Aloud* and *VIPs*—Review significant events that happened in the mid-1700s in the British colonies. Provide students with some background on Thomas Paine and *Common Sense*. Give students a copy of the *Common Sense* excerpts in **Handout 5.1**. Explain to students that their task will be to read one paragraph aloud, determine two VIPs from that specific paragraph, and write those VIPs in the margins beside the text. They may highlight or underline significant passages to help them decide what is most important. Model this by doing a Think Aloud with the first paragraph of the text with the class. Have students share what they think is important and write those VIPs in the margin as you are reading.

Next, divide the room into thirds and assign each third one section of the text:

- "Of Monarchy and Hereditary Succession"
- "Thoughts on the State of American Affairs"
- "On the Present Ability of America, With Some Miscellaneous Reflections"

Allow students to work with a partner to read their section of the text, choosing two VIPs from each paragraph. When two partner teams reading the same section are done, have them join and share what they chose as VIPs and why.

Next, reassemble the class into groups of six. Each group should have two students who read "Of Monarchy and Hereditary Succession," two who read "Thoughts on the State of American Affairs," and two who read "On the Present Ability of America, With Some Miscellaneous Reflections." In these new groups, have students share the VIPs from their section of *Common Sense* and help other students to understand that section. They should all take notes in the margins in order to understand all of the excerpts.

Make a Hypothesis: *Sketching Through the Text*—Once students have talked about each section of *Common Sense*, have them create a hypothesis that answers the organizing question. Give each group chart paper or poster board. Their task is to put the hypothesis on the top of the paper and draw five illustrations that represent evidence from all three parts of the text to support the hypothesis. Under the visuals, have students write key phrases from the text as evidence. Allow each group time to work and share their work at the end. Display these on your classroom walls so students will remember Paine's arguments as you discuss events leading to the American Revolution. Once these are displayed on the walls, have students discuss whether or not Paine's *Common Sense* seems similar to their brainstormed ideas from the lesson hook.

HANDOUT 5.1
EXCERPTS FROM THOMAS PAINE'S
(1776) *COMMON SENSE*

OF MONARCHY AND HEREDITARY SUCCESSION

But there is another and greater distinction, for which no truly natural or religious reason can be assigned, and that is, the distinction of men into KINGS and SUBJECTS. Male and female are the distinctions of nature, good and bad the distinctions of heaven; but how a race of men came into the world so exalted above the rest, and distinguished like some new species, is worth inquiring into, and whether they are the means of happiness or of misery to mankind . . .

To the evil of monarchy we have added that of hereditary succession; and as the first is a degradation and lessening of ourselves, so the second, claimed as a matter of right, is an insult and an imposition on posterity. For all men being originally equals, no ONE by BIRTH could have a right to set up his own family in perpetual preference to all others for ever, and though himself might deserve SOME decent degree of honours of his contemporaries, yet his descendants might be far too unworthy to inherit them. Secondly, as no man at first could possess any other public honours than were bestowed upon him, so the givers of those honours could have no power to give away the right of posterity. And though they might say, "We choose you for OUR head," they could not, without manifest injustice to their children, say, "that your children and your children's children shall reign over OURS forever." Because such an unwise, unjust, unnatural compact might (perhaps) in the next succession put them under the government of a rogue or a fool. Most wise men, in their private sentiments, have ever treated hereditary right with contempt; yet it is one of those evils, which when once established is not easily removed

THOUGHTS ON THE STATE OF AMERICAN AFFAIRS

We have boasted the protection of Great Britain, without considering, that her motive was INTEREST not ATTACHMENT; that she did not protect us from OUR ENEMIES on OUR ACCOUNT, but from HER ENEMIES on HER OWN ACCOUNT, from those who had no quarrel with us on any OTHER ACCOUNT, and who will always be our enemies on the SAME ACCOUNT. Let Britain wave her pretensions to the continent, or the continent throw off the dependence, and we should be at peace with France and Spain were they at war with Britain. It has lately been asserted in parliament, that the colonies have no relation to each other but through the parent country, i. e. that Pennsylvania and the Jerseys, and so on for the rest, are sister colonies by the way of England; this is certainly a very round-about way of proving relationship, but it is the nearest and only true way of proving enemyship, if I may so call it. France and Spain never were, nor perhaps ever will be our enemies as AMERICANS, but as our being the subjects of GREAT BRITAIN . . .

Much hath been said of the united strength of Britain and the colonies, that in conjunction they might bid defiance to the world. But this is mere presumption; the fate of war is uncertain, neither do the expressions mean anything; for this continent would never suffer itself to be drained of inhabitants, to support the British arms in either Asia, Africa, or Europe.

HANDOUT 5.1, CONTINUED

Besides what have we to do with setting the world at defiance? Our plan is commerce, and that, well attended to, will secure us the peace and friendship of all Europe; because, it is the interest of all Europe to have America a FREE PORT. Her trade will always be a protection,

and her barrenness of gold and silver secure her from invaders . . .

Small islands not capable of protecting themselves, are the proper objects for kingdoms to take under their care; but there is something very absurd, in supposing a continent to be perpetually governed by an island. In no instance hath nature made the satellite larger than its primary planet, and as England and America, with respect to each other, reverses the common order of nature, it is evident they belong to different systems; England to Europe, America to itself . . .

ON THE PRESENT ABILITY OF AMERICA, WITH SOME MISCELLANEOUS REFLECTIONS

TO CONCLUDE, however strange it may appear to some, or however unwilling they may be to think so, matters not, but many strong and striking reasons may be given, to shew, that nothing can settle our affairs so expeditiously as an open and determined declaration for independence. Some of which are,

FIRST. - It is the custom of nations, when any two are at war, for some other powers, not engaged in the quarrel, to step in as mediators, and bring about the preliminaries of a peace: but while America calls herself the Subject of Great Britain, no power, however well disposed she may be, can offer her mediation. Wherefore, in our present state we may quarrel on forever.

SECONDLY. - It is unreasonable to suppose, that France or Spain will give us any kind of assistance, if we mean only, to make use of that assistance for the purpose of repairing the breach, and strengthening the connection between Britain and America; because, those powers would be sufferers by the consequences.

THIRDLY. - While we profess ourselves the subjects of Britain, we must, in the eye of foreign nations, be considered as rebels. The precedent is somewhat dangerous to THEIR PEACE, for men to be in arms under the name of subjects; we, on the spot, can solve the paradox: but to unite resistance and subjection, requires an idea much too refined for common understanding.

FOURTHLY. - Were a manifesto to be published, and despatched to foreign courts, setting forth the miseries we have endured, and the peaceable methods we have ineffectually used for redress; declaring, at the same time, that not being able, any longer, to live happily or safely under the cruel disposition of the British court, we had been driven to the necessity of breaking off all connections with her; at the same time, assuring all such courts of our peaceable disposition towards them, and of our desire of entering into trade with them: Such a memorial would produce more good effects to this Continent, than if a ship were freighted with petitions to Britain . . .

Under our present denomination of British subjects, we can neither be received nor heard abroad: The custom of all courts is against us, and will be so, until, by an independance, we take rank with other nations . . .

LESSON 3

ORGANIZING QUESTION

How did the Declaration of Independence reflect colonists' dissatisfaction with their government?

STRATEGIES USED

Reciprocal Reading, Sketching Through the Text

MATERIALS NEEDED

1. One copy per student of the following:
   - ✓ Document: Declaration of Independence (1776), available at http://www.archives.gov/exhibits/charters/declaration_transcript.html
   - ✓ Sketching Through the Text: The Declaration of Independence graphic organizer (**Handout 5.2**)

2. One index card per student

LESSON PLAN

Lesson Hook: As students enter the classroom, have the following writing prompt on the board:

> Think of a time when someone close to you, such as a friend, family member, or teacher, really made you angry. On your index card, make a list of all the reasons you were angry and what he or she did wrong.

After 3 or 4 minutes, have students turn to the back of the index card and brainstorm ways they did or could have handled or solved the conflict. Have volunteers share their responses with the class.

The Organizing Question: Explain that students will do a close reading of the Declaration of Independence to answer the organizing question: How did the Declaration of Independence reflect colonists' dissatisfaction with their government?

Examine the Sources: *Reciprocal Reading*—Organize the class into groups of three and give students a copy of the Declaration of Independence. Divide the text into four or five sections or chunks, discuss the background of the document, and explain to students that their task is to read carefully to discover why the colonists declared independence against Great Britain. Read the first paragraph aloud with students and practice annotating the text for important ideas.

In groups of three, have students take turns reading a chunk of the document out loud. While the first student is reading aloud, the other two students should annotate important ideas from that section. At the end of each chunk of text, have students stop and share what they marked as important points and discuss any questions they have. Then switch readers and continue the process with the next chunk of text. Make sure all three students get to read. Circulate around the room, helping students with challenging vocabulary and making historical connections.

Make a Hypothesis: *Sketching Through the Text*—Once students have finished reading, annotating, and discussing each chunk of the Declaration of Independence, give them a copy of the Sketching Through the Text graphic organizer (**Handout 5.2**). As a group, have students use their annotations to create visuals for each section of the text that reflects the main idea of that section. For the section containing the list of grievances, they should design six visuals that capture the most important complaints against the king. Once students have created their sketches, have them write a hypothesis on the graphic organizer that answers the organizing question. Allow students to share their hypotheses and give supporting evidence from the text to explain their reasoning. These graphic organizers could be collected as a formative assessment for this lesson.

HANDOUT 5.2
SKETCHING THROUGH THE TEXT:
THE DECLARATION OF INDEPENDENCE

Directions: For each section of the document, create visuals in the boxes that represent the most important points from that section of the text.

Paragraph 1:

Paragraph 2:

List of Grievances:

HANDOUT 5.2, CONTINUED

Paragraph 3:

Paragraph 4:

Paragraph 5:

My Hypothesis:

1783-1800

CHAPTER 6

THE NEW NATION

> To all general purposes we have uniformly been one people each individual citizen everywhere enjoying the same national rights, privileges, and protection.—John Jay, 1787, Federalist No. 2

HISTORICAL BACKGROUND: WHAT DO I NEED TO KNOW?

After declaring independence, Americans faced three pressing, interrelated issues in creating a new national government: their relationship to each other, slavery, and the process of creating a legitimate government.

Most Americans, whatever their political leanings, believed in the political theory of republicanism, which incorporated three main ideas. The first was that governments always seek to take more power at the expense of the people—if not kept limited and restrained. Second, the best leaders would be those who would not personally benefit from power. Finally, those leaders should have "virtue," or a willingness to sacrifice themselves and their interests for the benefit of the public good.

The colonies created a formal government in 1781 through the Articles of Confederation. They gave the national government the power to wage war, conduct foreign relations, and coin money. In a reflection of Americans' fears of centralized power, this new confederation had no power to levy taxes or enforce laws and had no executive branch. States could issue currency and impose tariffs on each other. Most power was left to the states, which the Articles declared "sovereign."

Fear of national authority led to more power in the state legislatures, which became increasingly filled with non-elites marginalized during the colonial era. These ordinary people organized into groups of special interests eager to use the power of state government to benefit themselves and their constituents. Colonial elites believed that these kinds of organizations—called "factions" in the 18th century and "political parties" in the 21st—contradicted the spirit of virtue and therefore threatened the stability of the new nation. The inability of the Confederation Congress to effectively address postwar problems highlighted structural problems in the Articles.

Led by James Madison, the Constitutional Convention of 1787 authored a new Constitution. No longer able to coin money, conduct diplomacy, levy tariffs, or to claim sovereignty, the states would surrender most real power to the new federal government. The new plan for government met with a great deal of opposition and compromise. Proslavery Southerners forced an agreement to count slaves as three-fifths of a person for the purposes of taxation, while antislavery activists gained passage of a compromise that allowed Congress to vote to end the slave trade 20 years after ratification. Small states worried that larger states would dominate this powerful central government. The Great Compromise created a bicameral legislature, with the House determined by population and each state contributing two representatives to the Senate. The Electoral College was a compromise between those who wanted a popularly elected president and others who feared that uneducated voters would not be capable of picking someone with "virtue." In all, the new Constitution placed a great deal of power in the hands of the people, while a system of checks and balances prevented them from exercising it.

Once complete, the document stirred up a national debate between Federalist proponents of the new Constitution and Anti-Federalists, who were opposed to the power being taken from the states. Proponents agreed to support the ratification of a series of amendments, called the Bill of Rights, intended to protect some liberties that Anti-Federalists considered not clear enough in the body of the Constitution. In June 1788, the Constitution became the law of the land. George Washington, widely respected by both sides in the debate, was elected president of the new nation, taking office in March 1789.

STANDARDS ADDRESSED

NCHS U.S. History Content Standards, Grades 5–12:

- The institutions and practices of government created during the Revolution and how they were revised between 1787 and 1815 to create the foundation of the American political system based on the U.S. Constitution and the Bill of Rights

CCHS for Literacy in History/Social Studies, Grades 6–8:

- Determine the meaning of words and phrases as they are used in a text, including vocabulary specific to domains related to history/social studies.
- Describe how a text presents information (e.g., sequentially, comparatively, causally).
- Determine the central ideas or information of a primary or secondary source; provide an accurate summary of the source distinct from prior knowledge or opinions.

LESSON 1

ORGANIZING QUESTION

How does the Preamble of the United States Constitution lay the foundation for purposes of the U.S. government?

STRATEGIES USED

Concept Map, Frayer Model, Text Annotation

MATERIALS NEEDED

1. One copy per student of the source (or a class set of iPads or computers to access an electronic version) of The United States Constitution, available at http://www.archives.gov/exhibits/charters/constitution_transcript.html
2. One copy per student of Preamble Phrases Frayer Model (**Handout 6.1**)

LESSON PLAN

Lesson Hook: *Concept Map*—Write the word "government" on the board in big letters. Have students draw a concept map in their notes with "government" written in the middle circle. Ask them to brainstorm as many components or purposes of government as possible and to add the lines and ideas on their concept map. After about 3 minutes, have students compare their concept map with a partner to find overlaps and missing ideas. As students share their ideas with the class, make a class concept map on the board that shows purposes and parts of government.

The Organizing Question: Tell students that they will examine the Constitution of the U.S. for answers to the organizing question: How does the Preamble to the United States Constitution lay the foundation for purposes of the U.S. government?

Examine the Sources: *Frayer Model*—Display the text of the Preamble to the Constitution on a screen and read it aloud. Give every student a copy of **Handout 6.1**. Display a sample with the phrase "to form a more perfect union" written in the center circle. Model for students how to complete the four boxes of the organizer to develop a thorough understanding of the phrase. Next, divide students into groups and assign each group a phrase from the Preamble to complete on their own graphic organizers:

1. "establish justice"
2. "insure domestic tranquility"
3. "provide for the common defense"
4. "promote the general welfare"
5. "secure the blessings of liberty for ourselves and our posterity"

When completed, have students share their organizers with the class, so everyone understands the purposes of government described in the Preamble. Write the phrases on the board as they present them. Compare and contrast these with the ideas from the lesson hook.

Text Annotation—While students are still in their groups, assign each group an article of the Constitution to examine thoroughly. (*Note:* Based on group size and reading abilities of the students, combine articles four through seven and/or split the first three articles into chunks, if needed.) As they read, have them annotate the document for important ideas and powers provided to each branch. Allow each group time to read and discuss the main provisions in their article.

Make a Hypothesis: As students finish discussing their assigned article, have them answer the organizing question. Ask them to use the back of **Handout 6.1** to list examples of where they see the purposes of government from the Preamble discussed in their particular article. Allow time for students to share their findings and lists. End class with a discussion of whether or not students feel the writers of the Constitution effectively developed a plan for government that met the purposes of the Preamble.

HANDOUT 6.1
PREAMBLE PHRASES FRAYER MODEL

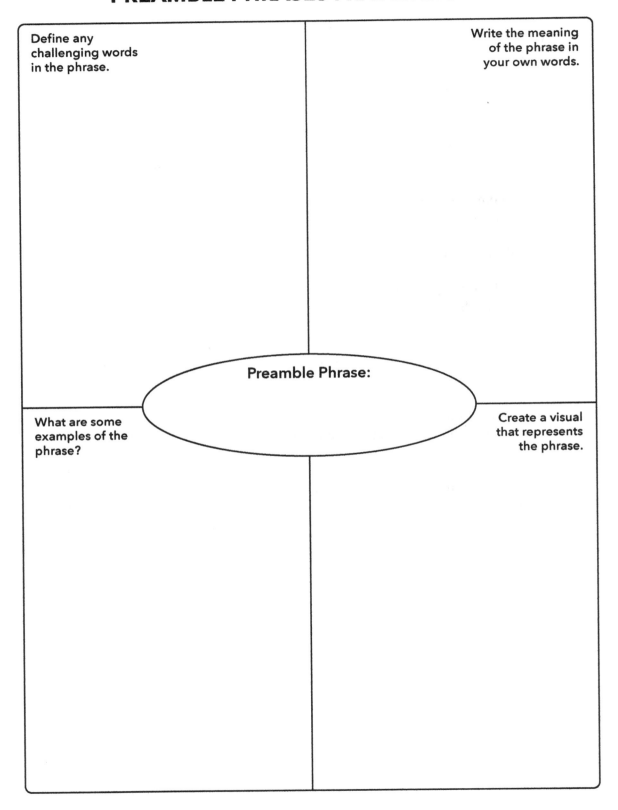

Define any challenging words in the phrase.

Write the meaning of the phrase in your own words.

Preamble Phrase:

What are some examples of the phrase?

Create a visual that represents the phrase.

LESSON 2

ORGANIZING QUESTION

How does the Bill of Rights help guarantee freedoms?

STRATEGIES USED

Talking Drawings, Reciprocal Teaching

MATERIALS NEEDED

1. One copy per student of the following:
    ✓ Government Document: Bill of Rights, U.S. Constitution, available at http://www.archives.gov/exhibits/charters/bill_of_rights_transcript.html
    ✓ Amendment Graphic Organizer (**Handout 6.2**)

2. Blank paper and markers or colored pencils for each student

LESSON PLAN

Lesson Hook: *Talking Drawings*—Give each student a blank piece of paper and markers or pencils. As a lesson hook and preassessment, have students write the phrase "My Rights" on the top of the paper. Give them 5–7 minutes to draw a picture of all the rights they think they have as U. S. citizens. As students share responses, ask them where these rights come from.

The Organizing Question: Explain that they will do a close reading of the Bill of Rights in order to answer the organizing question: How does the Bill of Rights help guarantee freedoms?

Examine the Sources: *Reciprocal Teaching*—Divide the class into groups of five. Depending on class size, assign each group two of the amendments. Give each student a copy of **Handout 6.2**. Either assign or have students choose one of the following roles and corresponding task. The Connector is the most challenging role if you want to differentiate these tasks.

- Reader: Read your assigned amendment loudly and clearly for your group.

- Summarizer: Explain the rights that are guaranteed in the amendment.
- Connector: Make connections between the rights guaranteed in the amendment and previous conflicts or events in history. Also, lead the group in brainstorming ways the amendment might affect your life today.
- Artist: Create a visual that represents the rights in the amendment.
- Reporter: Share your group's summary, connections, and visuals with the class.

Allow students time to read and discuss one amendment at a time. Each student should use the graphic organizer to complete his or her assigned task and then share the work with the group. Have each group reporter explain the amendments, connections, and show visuals while the class completes the graphic organizer.

Make a Hypothesis: Once all students have presented their amendments, assign the organizing question as a writing prompt to use as a formative assessment for the lesson. Allow students to use their graphic organizers, if needed, to get specific examples as evidence. End class with students looking back at their Talking Drawings "My Rights" pictures to see what they left out from the content discussed in today's lesson. Have them add images as needed.

HANDOUT 6.2
AMENDMENT GRAPHIC ORGANIZER

Amendment	What are my rights and freedoms?	Making Connections to History: What have we studied so far that made this amendment necessary?	Making Connections to My Life: Because of this amendment, as a citizen of the U.S., I can . . .

LESSON 3

ORGANIZING QUESTION

How did George Washington's "Farewell Address" outline a vision for the future of the United States?

STRATEGIES USED

Quick Write, Think Aloud, Very Important Points (VIPs)

MATERIALS NEEDED

1. One copy per student of Excerpts From George Washington's (1796) "Farewell Address" (**Handout 6.3**)
2. White chart paper and markers for each group

LESSON PLAN

Lesson Hook: *Quick Write*—Give students 10 minutes to complete the following writing task in their notebooks. Prompt them to think and write about current issues in the United States.

> If you could give advice to the people of the United States about ways to make the country prosper for the next decade, what advice would you give?

Allow students to share responses and list different themes or topics on the board.

The Organizing Question: Explain that they will analyze excerpts of George Washington's 1796 "Farewell Address" to answer the organizing question: How did George Washington's "Farewell Address" outline a vision for the future of the United States?

Examine the Sources: Explain to students George Washington's decision to retire from the presidency and return to Mount Vernon. Introduce his "Farewell Address" speech and his concern for the "factions" that were developing in the United States. Challenge students to work together and read the excerpts in

Handout 6.3 carefully to interpret the advice Washington was giving to the American people in his speech.

Think Aloud—Because the language and vocabulary of the speech may be challenging to students, read aloud the first excerpt in **Handout 6.3** with the class, share your process for figuring out difficult phrases, and model how to analyze vocabulary words through context clues. Annotate the text in the margins by writing the main ideas. Have students write the main ideas in the margins and add their thoughts to the analysis of the introduction. Before dividing into groups, make sure students understand the introduction and purpose of the "Farewell Address."

Very Important Points—Divide the class into six groups and assign each group an excerpt from the speech (excerpts two through seven). Explain that their task is to read and analyze their specific excerpt, to determine three VIPs Washington made in that section, and to write those three VIPs in the margins of the text. Students can take turns reading aloud and helping each other figure out difficult vocabulary words and phrases. After students finish, have each group choose a speaker to share the VIPs with the class. The class should take notes as each group presents the information.

Make a Hypothesis: Once all of the groups explain the VIPs from their section, have students work together to create a poster that answers the organizing question. Require them to create three or four visuals that represent phrases from the text. Depending on time constraints, have groups share their products and discuss similarities and differences in the content of Washington's "Farewell Address" with their advice to the current American people from the lesson hook section.

HANDOUT 6.3
EXCERPTS FROM GEORGE WASHINGTON'S "FAREWELL ADDRESS" (1796)

EXCERPT 1

Friends and Fellow Citizens:

The period for a new election of a citizen to administer the executive government of the United States being not far distant, and the time actually arrived when your thoughts must be employed in designating the person who is to be clothed with that important trust, it appears to me proper, especially as it may conduce to a more distinct expression of the public voice, that I should now apprise you of the resolution I have formed, to decline being considered among the number of those out of whom a choice is to be made.

I beg you, at the same time, to do me the justice to be assured that this resolution has not been taken without a strict regard to all the considerations appertaining to the relation which binds a dutiful citizen to his country; and that in withdrawing the tender of service, which silence in my situation might imply, I am influenced by no diminution of zeal for your future interest, no deficiency of grateful respect for your past kindness, but am supported by a full conviction that the step is compatible with both . . .

I rejoice that the state of your concerns, external as well as internal, no longer renders the pursuit of inclination incompatible with the sentiment of duty or propriety, and am persuaded, whatever partiality may be retained for my services, that, in the present circumstances of our country, you will not disapprove my determination to retire.

The impressions with which I first undertook the arduous trust were explained on the proper occasion. In the discharge of this trust, I will only say that I have, with good intentions, contributed towards the organization and administration of the government the best exertions of which a very fallible judgment was capable. Not unconscious in the outset of the inferiority of my qualifications, experience in my own eyes, perhaps still more in the eyes of others, has strengthened the motives to diffidence of myself; and every day the increasing weight of years admonishes me more and more that the shade of retirement is as necessary to me as it will be welcome. Satisfied that if any circumstances have given peculiar value to my services, they were temporary, I have the consolation to believe that, while choice and prudence invite me to quit the political scene, patriotism does not forbid it.

. . . Here, perhaps, I ought to stop. But a solicitude for your welfare, which cannot end but with my life, and the apprehension of danger, natural to that solicitude, urge me, on an occasion like the present, to offer to your solemn contemplation, and to recommend to your frequent review, some sentiments which are the result of much reflection, of no inconsiderable observation, and which appear to me all-important to the permanency of your felicity as a people. These will be offered to you with the more freedom, as you can only see in them the disinterested warnings of a parting friend, who can possibly have no personal motive to bias his counsel. Nor can I forget, as an encouragement to it, your indulgent reception of my sentiments on a former and not dissimilar occasion.

HANDOUT 6.3, CONTINUED

EXCERPT 2

. . . that your union and brotherly affection may be perpetual; that the free Constitution, which is the work of your hands, may be sacredly maintained; that its administration in every department may be stamped with wisdom and virtue; that, in fine, the happiness of the people of these States, under the auspices of liberty, may be made complete by so careful a preservation and so prudent a use of this blessing as will acquire to them the glory of recommending it to the applause, the affection, and adoption of every nation which is yet a stranger to it . . .

To the efficacy and permanency of your Union, a government for the whole is indispensable. No alliance, however strict, between the parts can be an adequate substitute; they must inevitably experience the infractions and interruptions which all alliances in all times have experienced. Sensible of this momentous truth, you have improved upon your first essay, by the adoption of a constitution of government better calculated than your former for an intimate union, and for the efficacious management of your common concerns. This government, the offspring of our own choice, uninfluenced and unawed, adopted upon full investigation and mature deliberation, completely free in its principles, in the distribution of its powers, uniting security with energy, and containing within itself a provision for its own amendment, has a just claim to your confidence and your support.

EXCERPT 3

The unity of government which constitutes you one people is also now dear to you. It is justly so, for it is a main pillar in the edifice of your real independence, the support of your tranquility at home, your peace abroad; of your safety; of your prosperity; of that very liberty which you so highly prize. But as it is easy to foresee that, from different causes and from different quarters, much pains will be taken, many artifices employed to weaken in your minds the conviction of this truth.

The name of American, which belongs to you in your national capacity, must always exalt the just pride of patriotism more than any appellation derived from local discriminations. With slight shades of difference, you have the same religion, manners, habits, and political principles. You have in a common cause fought and triumphed together; the independence and liberty you possess are the work of joint counsels, and joint efforts of common dangers, sufferings, and successes.

The North, in an unrestrained intercourse with the South, protected by the equal laws of a common government, finds in the productions of the latter great additional resources of maritime and commercial enterprise and precious materials of manufacturing industry. The South, in the same intercourse, benefiting by the agency of the North, sees its agriculture grow and its commerce expand . . . The East, in a like intercourse with the West, already finds, and in the progressive improvement of interior communications by land and water, will more and more find a valuable vent for the commodities which it brings from abroad, or manufactures at home. The West derives from the East supplies requisite to its growth and comfort, and, what is perhaps of

HANDOUT 6.3, CONTINUED

still greater consequence, it must of necessity owe the secure enjoyment of indispensable outlets for its own productions to the weight, influence, and the future maritime strength of the Atlantic side of the Union, directed by an indissoluble community of interest as one nation.

EXCERPT 4

While, then, every part of our country thus feels an immediate and particular interest in union, all the parts combined cannot fail to find in the united mass of means and efforts greater strength, greater resource, proportionably greater security from external danger, a less frequent interruption of their peace by foreign nations; and, what is of inestimable value, they must derive from union an exemption from those broils and wars between themselves, which so frequently afflict neighboring countries not tied together by the same governments, which their own rival ships alone would be sufficient to produce, but which opposite foreign alliances, attachments, and intrigues would stimulate and embitter. Hence, likewise, they will avoid the necessity of those overgrown military establishments which, under any form of government, are inauspicious to liberty, and which are to be regarded as particularly hostile to republican liberty. In this sense it is that your union ought to be considered as a main prop of your liberty, and that the love of the one ought to endear to you the preservation of the other.

EXCERPT 5

In contemplating the causes which may disturb our Union, it occurs as matter of serious concern that any ground should have been furnished for characterizing parties by geographical discriminations, Northern and Southern, Atlantic and Western; whence designing men may endeavor to excite a belief that there is a real difference of local interests and views. One of the expedients of party to acquire influence within particular districts is to misrepresent the opinions and aims of other districts. You cannot shield yourselves too much against the jealousies and heartburnings which spring from these misrepresentations; they tend to render alien to each other those who ought to be bound together by fraternal affection . . .

This spirit, unfortunately, is inseparable from our nature, having its root in the strongest passions of the human mind. It exists under different shapes in all governments, more or less stifled, controlled, or repressed; but, in those of the popular form, it is seen in its greatest rankness, and is truly their worst enemy.

The alternate domination of one faction over another, sharpened by the spirit of revenge, natural to party dissension, which in different ages and countries has perpetrated the most horrid enormities, is itself a frightful despotism. But this leads at length to a more formal and permanent despotism.

EXCERPT 6

Of all the dispositions and habits which lead to political prosperity, religion and morality are indispensable supports. In vain would that man claim the tribute of patrio-

HANDOUT 6.3, CONTINUED

tism, who should labor to subvert these great pillars of human happiness, these firmest props of the duties of men and citizens. The mere politician, equally with the pious man, ought to respect and to cherish them. A volume could not trace all their connections with private and public felicity. Let it simply be asked: Where is the security for property, for reputation, for life, if the sense of religious obligation desert the oaths which are the instruments of investigation in courts of justice? And let us with caution indulge the supposition that morality can be maintained without religion. Whatever may be conceded to the influence of refined education on minds of peculiar structure, reason and experience both forbid us to expect that national morality can prevail in exclusion of religious principle.

As a very important source of strength and security, cherish public credit. One method of preserving it is to use it as sparingly as possible, avoiding occasions of expense by cultivating peace, but remembering also that timely disbursements to prepare for danger frequently prevent much greater disbursements to repel it, avoiding likewise the accumulation of debt, not only by shunning occasions of expense, but by vigorous exertion in time of peace to discharge the debts which unavoidable wars may have occasioned, not ungenerously throwing upon posterity the burden which we ourselves ought to bear . . . To facilitate to them the performance of their duty, it is essential that you should practically bear in mind that towards the payment of debts there must be revenue; that to have revenue there must be taxes; that no taxes can be devised which are not more or less inconvenient and unpleasant; that the intrinsic embarrassment, inseparable from the selection of the proper objects (which is always a choice of difficulties), ought to be a decisive motive for a candid construction of the conduct of the government in making it, and for a spirit of acquiescence in the measures for obtaining revenue, which the public exigencies may at any time dictate.

EXCERPT 7

Observe good faith and justice towards all nations; cultivate peace and harmony with all. Religion and morality enjoin this conduct; and can it be, that good policy does not equally enjoin it? It will be worthy of a free, enlightened, and at no distant period, a great nation, to give to mankind the magnanimous and too novel example of a people always guided by an exalted justice and benevolence . . .

So likewise, a passionate attachment of one nation for another produces a variety of evils. Sympathy for the favorite nation, facilitating the illusion of an imaginary common interest in cases where no real common interest exists, and infusing into one the enmities of the other, betrays the former into a participation in the quarrels and wars of the latter without adequate inducement or justification. It leads also to concessions to the favorite nation of privileges denied to others which is apt doubly to injure the nation making the concessions; by unnecessarily parting with what ought to have been retained, and by exciting jealousy, ill-will, and a disposition to retaliate, in the parties from whom equal privileges are withheld. And it gives to ambitious, corrupted, or deluded citizens (who devote themselves to the favorite nation), facility to betray or sacrifice the interests of their own country, without odium, sometimes even with pop-

HANDOUT 6.3, CONTINUED

ularity; gilding, with the appearances of a virtuous sense of obligation, a commendable deference for public opinion, or a laudable zeal for public good, the base or foolish compliances of ambition, corruption, or infatuation.

As avenues to foreign influence in innumerable ways, such attachments are particularly alarming to the truly enlightened and independent patriot. How many opportunities do they afford to tamper with domestic factions, to practice the arts of seduction, to mislead public opinion, to influence or awe the public councils? Such an attachment of a small or weak towards a great and powerful nation dooms the former to be the satellite of the latter . . .

It is our true policy to steer clear of permanent alliances with any portion of the foreign world; so far, I mean, as we are now at liberty to do it; for let me not be understood as capable of patronizing infidelity to existing engagements. I hold the maxim no less applicable to public than to private affairs, that honesty is always the best policy. I repeat it, therefore, let those engagements be observed in their genuine sense. But, in my opinion, it is unnecessary and would be unwise to extend them.

1803-1850

CHAPTER 7

WESTWARD EXPANSION

> In all your intercourse with the natives, treat them in the most friendly & conciliatory manner which their own conduct will admit; allay all jealousies as to the object of your journey, satisfy them of its innocence, make them acquainted with the position, extent character, peaceable & commercial dispositions of the US, of our wish to be neighborly, friendly, & useful to them, & of our dispositions to a commercial intercourse with them . . . —Thomas Jefferson, Letter to Meriwether Lewis, 1803

HISTORICAL BACKGROUND: WHAT DO I NEED TO KNOW?

Settlers coming to colonial North America had access to land on a scale that Europeans could hardly imagine, and open access to land was a key feature of the American psyche. The new Confederation government assumed control of territory west of the Appalachians and passed a series of Western Ordinances in 1784, 1785, and 1787—the greatest achievement of the Confederation period. The laws guaranteed western settlers basic political and legal rights and allowed a territory to be admitted to the Union on an equal basis with other states when it had a population of 60,000. By guaranteeing that westward migrants would not lose their rights as Americans when they left their home states, and providing for the quick sale of land, the Ordinances set the destiny of the nation in the west.

In 1803 Thomas Jefferson's administration negotiated the purchase of Spanish Louisiana, effectively doubling the size of the nation overnight. Unlike the 1760s, the U.S. faced only weak adversaries and so needed no strong military to defend its borders or to expand them. Settlers poured into the West, driven by a restlessness unprecedented in the history of the Western world. Americans frequently would move three or four times in a lifetime and over long distances.

The vast new territory was largely uncharted by non-Natives, so President Jefferson funded several exploratory missions. One of these groups, consisting of more than 30 men and officially titled the Corps of Discovery Expedition, left St. Louis in May 1804. Led by Captain Meriwether Lewis and Second Lieutenant William Clark, the Corps moved north through the Midwest and upper-midwest, reaching the Pacific Ocean in November 1805. That only one person died along the way was in no small part due to the help of Sacagawea, a Shoshone woman who served as a guide, interpreter, and diplomat for the Corps. The group's discoveries revolutionized Americans' understanding of the West, established diplomatic relations with more than 20 Indian nations, catalogued more than 300 new species of plants and animals, and added immeasurably to American scientific thought.

The American fixation on the West affected almost every aspect of life, even giving birth to a uniquely American school of art. Artists of the Hudson River School, which began in the 1820s, took inspiration from the seemingly immense scale of the American West, both drawing inspiration from it and helping shape Americans' attitudes about it. Paintings in this style typically showed people as miniscule and overshadowed by the vast expanse of nature, which was often portrayed as a Garden of Eden—a land of opportunity.

In the meantime, the second major gold rush in American history started in the 1820s in the southern Appalachian Mountains of Georgia. Although the Cherokee people owned the land, prospectors flocked to the area, while White planters began to covet the rich farmland elsewhere in protected Indian homeland. Over the protests of Native peoples and some Whites, the U.S. Congress passed the Indian Removal Act, forcing Native American nations to sign treaties giving up their land. Between 1831 and 1842, the U.S. Army removed more than 50,000 Native Americans along the Trail of Tears to Oklahoma. Some 10,000 died along the way as the West opened to further White settlement.

STANDARDS ADDRESSED

NCHS U.S. History Content Standards, Grades 5–12:

- United States territorial expansion between 1801 and 1861 and how it affected relations with external powers and Native Americans
- How the industrial revolution, increasing immigration, the rapid expanse of slavery, and the westward movement changed the lives of Americans and led toward regional tensions
- The extension, restriction, and reorganization of political democracy after 1800

CCSS for Literacy in History/Social Studies, Grades 6–8:

- Cite specific textual evidence to support analysis of primary and secondary sources.
- Determine the central ideas or information of a primary or secondary source; provide an accurate summary of the source distinct from prior knowledge or opinions.

LESSON 1

ORGANIZING QUESTION
What were the purposes of Lewis and Clark's expedition?

STRATEGIES USED
Turn and Talk, Sketching Through the Text

MATERIALS NEEDED
1. One copy per student of the following:
   - ✓ Supply List: Meriwether Lewis and William Clark's Expedition (National Geographic, n.d.a), available at http://www.national geographic.com/lewisandclark/resources.html
   - ✓ Letter: Thomas Jefferson (1803) to Meriwether Lewis, available at http://www.loc.gov/exhibits/lewisandclark/transcript57.html

2. Map of the Louisiana Purchase to project to students or have students view on their computers or tablets, available at http://www.docsteach. org/documents/594889/detail
3. Construction paper and markers

LESSON PLAN

Lesson Hook: *Turn and Talk*—Show students an online map of the Louisiana Purchase. Have them work with a partner on the following task:

> You have been given the task of exploring the territory displayed on the map called the Louisiana Purchase. You expect the trip to last a year or more, and you have about 40 people in your expedition. Make a list of supplies you will need to take on your journey.

Ask students to share their responses and list them on the board. Have them brainstorm what might be some possible challenges on this trip.

The Organizing Question: Explain that they will examine two primary sources to answer the organizing question: What were the purposes of Lewis and Clark's expedition?

Examine the Sources: Give students a copy of Lewis and Clark's expedition supplies. With the same partner from the Turn and Talk exercise, have them see how many of the supplies that they generated in the lesson hook were on the actual supply list. Have students share the similarities and differences in their list and Lewis and Clark's version.

Sketching Through the Text—Next, have student pairs combine to create groups of four. Give each group copies of Jefferson's (1803) letter to Meriwether Lewis, a piece of construction paper per group, and markers. Have the students take turns reading sections of the letter aloud and underlining the purposes of the expedition as they are mentioned.

Make a Hypothesis: When students are finished reading and underlining evidence, have them draw six pictures on their construction paper that represent answers to the organizing question, i.e., the purposes of Lewis and Clark's expedition. They must be able to explain their sketch with evidence from Jefferson's letter. Once all groups have completed their sketches and presented them to the class, end class with a final look and discussion of the expedition supply list. Ask students to give their opinion on whether or not Lewis and Clark packed adequate supplies to accomplish the expedition's purposes.

LESSON 2

ORGANIZING QUESTION

How did early 19th-century art reflect Americans' vision of the West?

STRATEGIES USED

Think Aloud, Gradual Release

MATERIALS NEEDED

1. Online versions of the following:
    - ✓ Photo gallery: Grand Tetons (National Park Service, n.d.a), available at http://www.nps.gov/grte/photosmultimedia/photogallery.htm
    - ✓ Photo gallery: Yellowstone (National Park Service, n.d.c), available at http://www.nps.gov/yell/photosmultimedia/photogallery.htm
    - ✓ Photo gallery: Yosemite National Park Photos (National Geographic, n.d.b), available at http://travel.nationalgeographic.com/travel/national-parks/yosemite-photos/
    - ✓ Painting: Thomas Cole's (1846) *The Mountain Ford*, available at http://www.metmuseum.org/toah/works-of-art/15.30.63

2. One copy per student of the Analyzing Photographs and Prints Guide, available at http://www.loc.gov/teachers/usingprimarysources/resources/Analyzing_Photographs_and_Prints.pdf
3. One color copy per group of each of the following:
    - ✓ Painting: Thomas Cole's (1836) *View from Mount Holyoke, Northampton, Massachusetts, After a Thunderstorm—The Oxbow*, available at http://www.metmuseum.org/toah/works-of-art/08.228
    - ✓ Painting: Asher Durand's (1849) *Kindred Spirits*, available at http://www.metmuseum.org/toah/works-of-art/L.2008.21
    - ✓ Painting: Asher Durand's (1845) *The Beeches*, available at http://www.metmuseum.org/toah/works-of-art/15.30.59
    - ✓ Painting: Asher Durand's (1855) *In the Woods*, available at http://www.metmuseum.org/toah/works-of-art/95.13.1
    - ✓ Painting: Albert Bierstadt's (1863) *The Rocky Mountains, Lander's Peak*, available at http://www.metmuseum.org/toah/works-of-art/07.123

LESSON PLAN

Lesson Hook: As students enter the classroom, display two or three scenic photographs of different U.S. national parks on a screen. Have students choose which of the locations they might want to visit and explain their reasons. Ask students to discuss what details they notice in the photos and what elements in the pictures would make them want to visit these scenic sites.

The Organizing Question: Explain that students will examine several paintings to gather clues to answer the organizing question: How did early 19th-century art reflect Americans' vision of the West?

Examine the Sources: *Gradual Release* and *Think Aloud*—Provide students with some background on the Hudson River School of artists and the types of works they created. Pass out copies of the Analyzing Photographs and Prints Guide to students. Display Thomas Cole's (1846) *The Mountain Ford* on a screen. Think aloud with students to model how to analyze artwork using the categories and questions on the Observe, Reflect, and Question sections of the Analyzing Photographs and Prints Guide.

We Do—When you get to the Question section on the guide, have students share their thinking about what they notice in the painting and what questions they have. Using the websites provided, try to help them find answers to the questions they generated. Ask them how this painting might help provide answers to the organizing question. Explain to students that now that they have analyzed a painting together, they will work in groups to analyze other paintings from the Hudson River School.

You Do—Divide the class into five groups and give each group a painting. Explain to students that they will examine their painting using the guide. As a group, have them write down answers to some of the questions in the Observe, Reflect, and Question sections in order to be prepared to share their analysis with the class.

Make a Hypothesis: Write the organizing question on the board. Ask students to write down examples of evidence that might help answer the organizing question as each group presents its artwork. Allow each group to show its painting and analysis notes. As a whole class, compose a list of how the six pieces of art examined in class help answer the question. Compare and contrast the purposes of the artwork with the photos and discussion points made in the lesson hook section. If time permits, a compare and contrast writing task could be a formative assessment for the lesson.

LESSON 3

ORGANIZING QUESTION
How are competing viewpoints reflected in the arguments for and against the Indian Removal Act?

STRATEGIES USED
Picture Prediction, Modified Jigsaw

MATERIALS NEEDED
1. One copy per student of the Viewpoints on Indian Removal Graphic Organizer (**Handout 7.1**)
2. An online version of any map of the Indian Removal Act and any painting of the Trail of Tears
3. Copies for each group of the following primary sources:
    ✓ Group 1: Speech: Excerpts From Andrew Jackson's (1830) "Second Annual Message to Congress" (**Handout 7.2**)
    ✓ Group 2: Letter: Excerpts From Chief John Ross (1836) of the Cherokee Nation's Letter to the Senate and House of Representatives (**Handout 7.3**)
    ✓ Group 3: Speech: Excerpts From Peleg Sprague's (1830) "Speech to Congress" (**Handout 7.4**)
    ✓ Group 4: Speech: Excerpts From John Forsyth's (1830) "Speech to Congress" (**Handout 7.5**)

LESSON PLAN

Lesson Hook: *Picture Prediction*—Begin the lesson by showing students any online painting of the Trail of Tears and a map of Indian Removal Act routes and resettlement areas. As students look at each image, have them write answers to the following questions in their notes:
- What do you think this painting/map portrays?
- What evidence from the image makes you think that?
- Based on this image, make a prediction about what the topic of today's lesson will be.

Allow students to share their reactions to the images and their lesson predictions.

The Organizing Question: Explain that they will examine four primary sources to answer the following question: How are competing viewpoints reflected in the arguments for and against the Indian Removal Act?

Examine the Sources: Begin the lesson with a brief introduction of the Indian Removal Act of 1830. Explain that there were competing viewpoints on the issue of Indian removal, and these documents will provide evidence to discover those views.

Expert groups: Divide the class into four groups and give every student a copy of **Handout 7.1.** Explain to students that they will become experts on one primary source, but by the end of the lesson, they will understand several arguments for and against Indian removal. Give students in each group a copy of the document from these sources:

- Group 1: (**Handout 7.2**)
- Group 2: (**Handout 7.3**)
- Group 3: (**Handout 7.4**)
- Group 4: (**Handout 7.5**)

Their expert group task is to closely read and annotate the document, looking for arguments either for or against Indian removal. If needed, model a paragraph from one of the sources to help students understand how to annotate difficult text for important ideas and how to complete the graphic organizer and record the main arguments from their source.

As these are challenging documents, encourage students to read and discuss one paragraph at a time. Circulate and help students with difficult phrasing, background knowledge, and vocabulary context clues as needed. After students complete the document and graphic organizer, assign each student a letter (e.g., a, b, c, d, e, etc., depending on how many students are in each expert group).

Home (or letter) groups: For the next part of the jigsaw, students will go to home or letter groups. All the "A" students, "B" students, and "C" students, for instance, should sit together. In that home group, they will have an expert on each of the four documents. Students should take turns sharing their document. Encourage them to explain the author, time period, and main arguments from their expert group discussions. The other students in the group should complete the graphic organizer in **Handout 7.1** with arguments for and against Indian removal.

Make a Hypothesis: After all students in the home groups have shared their sources, have them answer the last part of **Handout 7.1** by making a hypothesis with supporting data to answer the organizing question. Allow each group to report the hypothesis and data. Finish the lesson by returning to the two lesson hook images. Ask students to look at their initial predictions and elaborate on the meaning of those images based on the content learned from the four primary sources. An alternative lesson ending is to have students individually write responses to the questions at the end of **Handout 7.1**.

NAME:

DATE:

HANDOUT 7.1

VIEWPOINTS ON INDIAN REMOVAL GRAPHIC ORGANIZER

Arguments For	Source	Arguments Against
	Andrew Jackson's (1830) "State of the Union Address"	
	Letter from Cherokee Chief John Ross (1836) to Congress	
	Peleg Sprague's (1830) Speech to Congress	
	John Forsyth's (1830) Speech to Congress	

HANDOUT 7.1, CONTINUED

1. How are competing viewpoints reflected in the arguments for and against Indian Removal?

   _____

   _____

   _____

   _____

   _____

2. Our hypothesis is:

   _____

   _____

   _____

   _____

   _____

3. Our evidence to support the hypothesis is:

   _____

   _____

   _____

   _____

   _____

HANDOUT 7.2
EXCERPTS FROM ANDREW JACKSON'S (1830) "SECOND ANNUAL MESSAGE TO CONGRESS"

It gives me pleasure to announce to Congress that the benevolent policy of the Government, steadily pursued for nearly 30 years, in relation to the removal of the Indians beyond the white settlements is approaching to a happy consummation.

The consequences of a speedy removal will be important to the United States, to individual States, and to the Indians themselves. The pecuniary advantages which it promises to the Government are the least of its recommendations. It puts an end to all possible danger of collision between the authorities of the General and State Governments on account of the Indians. It will place a dense and civilized population in large tracts of country now occupied by a few savage hunters. By opening the whole territory between Tennessee on the north and Louisiana on the south to the settlement of the whites it will incalculably strengthen the SW frontier and render the adjacent States strong enough to repel future invasions without remote aid. It will relieve the whole State of Mississippi and the western part of Alabama of Indian occupancy, and enable those States to advance rapidly in population, wealth, and power. It will separate the Indians from immediate contact with settlements of whites; free them from the power of the States; enable them to pursue happiness in their own way and under their own rude institutions; will retard the progress of decay, which is lessening their numbers, and perhaps cause them gradually, under the protection of the Government and through the influence of good counsels, to cast off their savage habits and become an interesting, civilized, and Christian

Humanity has often wept over the fate of the aborigines of this country, and Philanthropy has been long busily employed in devising means to avert it, but its progress has never for a moment been arrested, and one by one have many powerful tribes disappeared from the earth . . . Philanthropy could not wish to see this continent restored to the condition in which it was found by our forefathers. What good man would prefer a country covered with forests and ranged by a few thousand savages to our extensive Republic, studded with cities, towns, and prosperous farms, embellished with all the improvements which art can devise or industry execute, occupied by more than 12,000,000 happy people, and filled with all the blessings of liberty, civilization, and religion?

The present policy of the Government is but a continuation of the same progressive change by a milder process. The tribes which occupied the countries now constituting the Eastern States were annihilated or have melted away to make room for the whites. The waves of population and civilization are rolling to the westward, and we now propose to acquire the countries occupied by the red men of the South and West by a fair exchange, and, at the expense of the United States, to send them to a land where their existence may be prolonged and perhaps made perpetual.

. . . And is it supposed that the wandering savage has a stronger attachment to his home than the settled, civilized Christian? Is it more afflicting to him to leave the graves of his fathers than it is to our brothers and children? Rightly considered, the policy of the General Government toward the red man is not only liberal, but generous. He is unwilling to submit to the laws of the States and mingle with their population. To save him from this alternative, or perhaps utter annihilation, the General Government kindly offers him a new home, and proposes to pay the whole expense of his removal and settlement.

HANDOUT 7.3
EXCERPTS FROM CHIEF JOHN ROSS (1836) OF THE CHEROKEE NATION'S LETTER TO THE SENATE AND HOUSE OF REPRESENTATIVES

. . . After the departure of the Delegation, a contract was made by the Rev. John F. Schermerhorn, and certain individual Cherokees, purporting to be a "treaty, concluded at New Echota, in the State of Georgia, on the 29th day of December, 1835, by General William Carroll and John F. Schermerhorn, commissioners on the part of the United States, and the chiefs, headmen, and people of the Cherokee tribes of Indians" . . . And now it is presented to us as a treaty, ratified by the Senate, and approved by the President [Andrew Jackson], and our acquiescence in its requirements demanded, under the sanction of the displeasure of the United States, and the threat of summary compulsion, in case of refusal . . .

By the stipulations of this instrument, we are despoiled of our private possessions, the indefeasible property of individuals. We are stripped of every attribute of freedom and eligibility for legal self-defence. Our property may be plundered before our eyes; violence may be committed on our persons; even our lives may be taken away, and there is none to regard our complaints. We are denationalized; we are disfranchised. We are deprived of membership in the human family! We have neither land nor home, nor resting place that can be called our own. And this is effected by the provisions of a compact which assumes the venerated, the sacred appellation of treaty . . .

The instrument in question is not the act of our Nation; we are not parties to its covenants; it has not received the sanction of our people. The makers of it sustain no office nor appointment in our Nation . . . And, therefore, we, the parties to be affected by the result, appeal with confidence to the justice, the magnanimity, the compassion, of your honorable bodies, against the enforcement, on us, of the provisions of a compact, in the formation of which we have had no agency.

In truth, our cause is your own; it is the cause of liberty and of justice; it is based upon your own principles, which we have learned from yourselves; for we have gloried to count your [George] Washington and your [Thomas] Jefferson our great teachers; we have read their communications to us with veneration; we have practised their precepts with success. And the result is manifest. The wildness of the forest has given place to comfortable dwellings and cultivated fields, stocked with the various domestic animals. Mental culture, industrious habits, and domestic enjoyments, have succeeded the rudeness of the savage state.

We have learned your religion also. We have read your Sacred books. Hundreds of our people have embraced their doctrines, practised the virtues they teach, cherished the hopes they awaken, and rejoiced in the consolations which they afford . . . For assuredly, we are not ignorant of our condition; we are not insensible to our sufferings. We feel them! We groan under their pressure! And anticipation crowds our breasts with sorrows yet to come. We are, indeed, an afflicted people! Our spirits are subdued! Despair has well nigh seized upon our energies!

But we speak to the representatives of a Christian country; the friends of justice; the patrons of the oppressed. And our hopes revive, and our prospects brighten, as we indulge the thought. On your sentence, our fate is suspended; prosperity or desolation depends on your word. To you, therefore, we look! Before your august assembly we present ourselves, in the attitude of deprecation, and of entreaty. On your kindness, on your humanity, on your compassion, on your benevolence, we rest our hopes. To you we address our reiterated prayers. Spare our people! Spare the wreck of our prosperity! Let not our deserted homes become the monuments of our desolation!

HANDOUT 7.4
EXCERPTS FROM PELEG SPRAGUE'S (1830) "SPEECH TO CONGRESS"

. . . I at present contend only that the Indians have a right to exist as a community, and to possess some spot of earth upon which to sustain that existence. That spot is their native land. If they have no claim there, they have no right anywhere. Georgia asserts that the lands belong to her—she must and she will have them—even by violence, if other means fail. This is a declaration of right to drive the Cherokees from the face of the earth; for if she is not bound to permit them to remain, no nation or people are bound to receive them. To that for which I now contend the Indians possess not only a natural, but also a legal and conventional right.

. . . Much has been said of their being untutored savages, as if that could dissolve our treaties! No one pretends that they are less cultivated now than when those treaties were made. Indeed, it is certain that they have greatly advanced in civilization; we see it in the very proofs introduced by the gentleman from Georgia to show their barbarism. He produced to the Senate a printed code of Cherokee laws, and a newspaper issued from a Cherokee press! Is there another instance of such production from any Indian nation? . . . Time will not permit me to dwell upon their advances in the arts of civilized life. It is known to have been great. They till the ground, manufacture for themselves, have workshops, a printing press, schools, churches, and a regularly organized Government.

. . . Whither are the Cherokees to go? What system has been matured for their security? What laws for their government? These questions are answered only by gilded promises in general terms; they are to become enlightened and civilized husbandmen. . . . They now live by the cultivation of the soil, and the mechanic arts. It is proposed to send them from their cotton fields, their farms, and their gardens, to a distant and an unsubdued wilderness—to make them tillers of the earth; to remove them from their looms, their workshops, their printing press, their schools, and churches, near the white settlements, in frowning forest, surrounded with naked savages—that they may become enlightened and civilized! We have pledged to them our protection; and, instead of shielding them where they now are, within our reach, under our own arm, we sent these natives of a southern clime to northern regions, amongst fierce and warlike barbarians. And what security do we propose to them? A new guarantee!! Who can look an Indian in the face, and say to him, we and our fathers, for more than forty years, have made to you the most solemn promises; we now violate and trample upon them all; but offer you, in their stead, another guarantee!

. . . Let us not compel them, by withdrawing the protection which we have pledged. Theirs must be the pain of departure, and the hazard of the change. They are men, and have the feelings and attachments of men; and if all the ties which bind them to their country and their homes are to be rent asunder, let it be by their own free hand. If they are to leave forever the streams in which they have drank, and the trees under which they have reclined; if the fires are never more to be lighted up in the council house of their chiefs, and must be quenched forever upon the domestic hearth, by the tears of the inmates, who have there joined the nuptial feast, and the funeral wail—if they are to look for the last time upon the land of their birth, which drank up the blood of their fathers, shed in its defence—and is mingled with the sacred dust of children and friends—to turn their aching vision to distant regions enveloped in darkness and surrounded by dangers—let it be by their own free choice, not by the coercion or a withdrawal of the protection of our plighted faith.

HANDOUT 7.5
EXCERPTS FROM JOHN FORSYTH'S (1830) "SPEECH TO CONGRESS"

. . . Although not reconciled to the project of Mr. Monroe's administration, I was convinced that the basis of that project—the removal of the Indians beyond the States and Territories— was the only mode by which the power of the General Government could be properly and exclusively exercised for their benefit. I do not believe that this removal will accelerate the civilization of the tribes. You might as reasonably expect that wild animals, incapable of being tamed in a park, would be domesticated by turning them loose in the forest . . . This desirable end cannot be obtained without destroying the tribal character, and subjecting the Indians, as individuals, to the regular action of well digested laws. Wild nature never was yet tamed but by coercive discipline.

The recent experiment made on the Arkansas has somewhat shaken my faith. It is understood that the Cherokees, who removed to that country in 1817–1818, with a view to continue the hunter's life, have advanced more rapidly than those who remained on this side of the Mississippi, in the arts of civilized life. Yet, doubting, as I do, the effect of this measure as a means of civilization, I shall vote for it, with a hope of relieving the States from a population useless and burthensome, and from a conviction that the physical condition of the Indians will be greatly improved by the change: a change not intended to be forced upon them, but to be the result of their own judgment, under the persuasions of those who are quite as anxious for their prosperity and tranquility, as the self-constituted guardians of their rights, who have filled this Hall with essays and pamphlets in their favor.

That all the Indians in the United States would be benefitted by their removal beyond the states, to a country appropriated for their exclusive residence, cannot be doubted by any dispassionate man who knows their condition. With one or two remarkable exceptions, all the tribes are rapidly diminishing in number . . . All these Indians, with the exception of the Cherokees in Georgia, are in a state of involuntary minority. Without industry, and without incentives to improvement, with the mark of degradation fixed upon them by State laws; without the control of their own resources, depending upon a precarious, because ill-directed, agriculture, they are little better than the wandering gypsies of the old world, living by beggary or plunder.

The United States are bound by compact to pay all the cost of extinguishing the Indian claim to lands lying within her limits. In the new States, the only benefit to be derived by the United States from the removal of the Indians is this: The lands occupied by them will be immediately subject to survey, sale, and settlement. For the old and for the new States, this important object will be gained: a race not admitted to be equal to the rest of the community; not governed as completely dependent; treated somewhat like human beings, but not admitted to be freemen; not yet entitled, and probably never to be entitled, to equal civil and political rights, will be humanely provided for.

. . . The Cherokee Government is in the hands of a few half-breeds and white men, who, through its instrumentality, regulate the affairs and control all the funds of the tribe. There is a press established, supported by those funds: a press established in a community of thirteen thousand souls, not five hundred of whom can read or write? The money which ought to be used to feed and clothe the common Indians, who are represented as half starved and naked wretches, is applied to the support of a printing press, to the establishment of exchanges of newspapers with the printers of the United States.

1850-1865

CHAPTER 8

SECTIONALISM AND CIVIL WAR

Both parties deprecated war, but one of them would make war rather than let the nation survive, and the other would accept war rather than let it perish. And the war came.—Abraham Lincoln, Second Inaugural Address, March 4, 1865

HISTORICAL BACKGROUND: WHAT DO I NEED TO KNOW?

The opening of the West that brought so much opportunity to the United States also nearly proved its undoing. Although most Americans in 1787 assumed that slavery would soon die off, the invention of the cotton gin brought new profitability to slave plantations, and slave owners felt the same westward pull as other Americans. Some Americans, however, began to argue that where slavery was legal, true opportunity was restricted to a very small elite. Whatever their feelings about African Americans, some White Americans began to equate slavery with backwardness and decided that it should be kept out of the new territories.

In 1819, Alabama entered the Union as a slave state, which balanced the number of free and slave states, and therefore, senators. Maine's petition for statehood in 1820 threatened to throw off the balance. In the Compromise of

1820, Congress agreed to admit Maine as a free state, Missouri as a slave state, and prohibited slavery in the Western territories north of the southern Missouri border.

The Compromise of 1850, an outgrowth of the results of the Mexican-American War, left the institution essentially intact, although it did bar the slave trade (but not slavery) in Washington, D.C., strengthened the Fugitive Slave Act, and admitted California as a free state. Far from pushing slavery into the background, the Compromise of 1850 brought slavery into the heart of American politics.

Congress passed the Kansas-Nebraska Act in 1854, which opened the territory to settlement, but also gave White male inhabitants the right to vote for or against slavery. This repeal of the Missouri Compromise caused outrage. Northern Whites blamed a supposed Southern White "slave power" who wanted to keep Black people in chains and force all other Americans to bow to their rule. For their part, Southern Whites believed that Northern antislavery activists were out to destroy their way of life.

For Whites in the slave states, the election of Abraham Lincoln, a Republican, to the presidency, signaled an immediate threat. Compromise, an essential feature of American politics, proved impossible and several Southern states immediately drew up declarations of secession modeled on the Declaration of Independence. As the war began, other slave states followed suit, believing that their passion for the cause would outweigh any material benefit Northern states might have.

Each year Congress took a census to determine congressional representation. The Census of 1860 (United States Census Bureau, 1860) revealed a startling trend: the South was falling behind in almost every important economic measure. Despite the profitability of slavery, the Southern states were producing fewer agricultural products and losing ground on manufacturing and railroad mileage. Although the population was rising everywhere, the number of White inhabitants in slave states was also declining relative to the non-slave states.

Despite prodding from antislavery activists, Lincoln's war plans followed a cautious policy of bringing the slave states back into the Union in any way possible. He eventually came to see the slavery issue as part of the strategy, and a major Union victory at Antietam in 1862 allowed him to issue the Emancipation Proclamation. What had been a war to defeat the South immediately became a war to free the slaves, regardless of the reasons for which individuals might fight. When Lincoln delivered his Second Inaugural Address, 5 weeks before Union victory and his own death, he noted that, "All knew that this interest was somehow the cause of the war." Although Lincoln had not set out to do it, the end of the war brought the end of the institution of slavery.

STANDARDS ADDRESSED

NCHS U.S. History Content Standards, Grades 5–12:
- How the industrial revolution, increasing immigration, the rapid expanse of slavery, and the westward movement changed the lives of Americans and led toward regional tensions
- The causes of the Civil War
- The course and character of the Civil War and its effects on the American people

CCSS for Literacy in History/Social Studies, Grade 6–8:
- Cite specific textual evidence to support analysis of primary and secondary sources.
- Identify aspects of a text that reveal an author's point of view or purposes (e.g., loaded language, inclusion or avoidance of particular facts).
- Integrate visual information (e.g. in charts, graphs, photographs, videos, or maps) with other information in print and digital texts.

LESSON 1

ORGANIZING QUESTION

Why did some states secede from the Union?

STRATEGIES USED

Think Aloud, Reciprocal Teaching, Sketching Through the Text

MATERIALS NEEDED

1. An online version of the following to display on a screen: *Georgia Secession* (Confederate States of America, 1861b), available at http://avalon.law.yale.edu/19th_century/csa_geosec.asp

2. Six or seven copies of the following:
   ✓ Government document: *A Declaration of the Immediate Causes Which Induce and Justify the Secession of the State of Mississippi from the Federal Union* (Confederate States of America, n.d.), available at http://avalon.law.yale.edu/19th_century/csa_missec.asp
   ✓ Government document: *Declaration of the Immediate Causes Which Induce and Justify the Secession of South Carolina from the Federal Union* (Confederate States of America, 1860), available at http://avalon.law.yale.edu/19th_century/csa_scarsec.asp
   ✓ Government document: *A Declaration of the Causes Which Impel the State of Texas to Secede From the Federal Union* (Confederate States of America, 1861a), available at http://avalon.law.yale.edu/19th_century/csa_texsec.asp

3. Chart paper, highlighters, and markers for each group

LESSON PLAN

Lesson Hook: Write the following question on the board and have students respond by writing thoughts in their notes:

Do you think states have the right to leave the U.S. if they don't agree with the policies of the government or its leaders?

Allow students to share ideas and ask them to think of other examples in history when this happened or how the Constitution might address this question.

The Organizing Question: Explain that students will examine secession documents from four Southern states to find an answer to the organizing question: Why did some states secede from the Union?

Examine the Sources: *Think Aloud*—Explain to students that they will work with a group to analyze the secession documents using these four reciprocal teaching roles:

- Reader: Read the section loudly and clearly for your group.
- Summarizer: Explain the main reasons for secession from this section.
- Connector: Make connections between the text and previous conflicts or events in history.
- Artist: Create a visual in the margins that represents the reason for secession in this section.

Display an online version of Georgia's secession document. In order to prepare them for the challenging texts and their roles, use this Georgia secession document as an example. Read the first section aloud and model for students how to analyze the document using the four roles above. Take notes on the document and create a visual in the margin as you complete each section. Continue through the Georgia document, allowing the students to follow along and prompting their discussion using each of the roles. At the end of the document, ask students why Georgia seceded from the union and have them assess whether or not those were valid reasons.

Reciprocal Teaching—Divide students into groups of four and give each group a copy of a state secession document from Mississippi, South Carolina, or Texas. Have students divide their document into four different sections or chunks. Either assign or have students choose one of the following roles and corresponding tasks. The Connector is the most challenging role if you want to differentiate these tasks.

Have students read the first section of their document. Encourage them to highlight or write in the margins important ideas from the reading so they will be prepared for the discussion. After each section, students should stop reading and discuss the section by using their assigned roles. Then, students should switch roles with the person to their right and read and discuss the next section.

Make a Hypothesis: *Sketching Through the Text*—Once students finish reading and discussing their document, have them work as a group to create a poster with the state name at the top and three or four sketches that represent that state's main reasons for secession. They may use some of the visuals that were created by the artist. Under each visual, have students write words or phrases from the text that are evidence to support their hypotheses. Allow time for groups to create and share their posters with the rest of the class. End the class by assigning the organizing question as a writing prompt to use as an assessment for the lesson. Allow students to use the posters, if needed, to get specific examples as evidence.

LESSON 2

ORGANIZING QUESTION

Which side was better prepared to fight the Civil War?

STRATEGIES USED

Brainstorming, Role-Play

MATERIALS NEEDED

1. An online version of any 1860 U.S. map (A variety are available online.)
    ✓ One copy per student of Census of 1860 (**Handout 8.1**)

2. Chart paper and markers for the North and South

LESSON PLAN

Lesson Hook: *Brainstorming*—Ask students to take 5 minutes and brainstorm answers to this question in their notes. When they are finished, make a class list of answers on the board.

In 2014, what resources are needed for a country to fight a war?

The Organizing Question: Explain that students will pretend to be war planners for either the North or South. Their goal is to examine census data from 1860 to assess how well prepared their side is to fight a war. At the end of the lesson, the class will use the census data to answer the organizing question: Which side was better prepared to fight the Civil War?

Examine the Sources: *Brainstorming*—Begin this section of the lesson by having students brainstorm a list of what would be needed to fight a war in the mid-1800s. Write their list of resources on the board. Prompt their thinking by showing a map of the U.S. from 1860. Using the map, have students predict what war strategies might be effective to conquer the enemy. Ask them what resources might be needed to make these strategies successful. Once a thorough list is created on the board, explain that the origin, purpose, and types of data collected in the U.S. Census will help them determine resources available for waging war.

Role-Play—Divide the class into two large groups. Half of the class will be the North, and the other half will be the South. The year is 1860, and students are war planners charged with the task of assessing their side's resources available for fighting a war. Before dividing into groups, model how to read the census data and how to determine what the implications might be for war planning.

Next, within the large North and South groups, assign the students into six smaller groups (three North and three South), and give each group **Handout 8.1** to analyze. Have each small group look at the data to determine what the chart is showing. Encourage them to make notes on the side of their census table. After a few minutes, have the North and South groups meet as a whole, share their findings, and determine strengths and weaknesses for war preparedness. Next, have the North and South groups face each other and share the data, predicting possible strengths and weaknesses compared to the list of resources needed on the board. Write the strengths and weaknesses on the board as groups report them.

Make a Hypothesis: Ask students to individually write a hypothesis on which side was better prepared to fight the Civil War. They must use evidence from the census data and class discussions to support the hypothesis. Allow students to share their hypotheses and predict what they think might happen in the war based on the census data.

HANDOUT 8.1
CENSUS OF 1860

	New York	Massachusetts	Ohio	Georgia	Virginia	South Carolina
Transportation						
Railroad Mileage	2,701.84	1,272.96	2,999.45	1,404.22	1,771.16	987.97
Agriculture						
Improved Farmland (Acres)	14,358,403	2,155,512	12,625,394	8,062,758	11,437,821	4,572,060
Horses	503,725	47,786	625,346	130,771	287,579	81,125
Mules	1,553	108	7,194	101,069	41,015	56,456
Wheat (bushels)	8,681,105	119,783	15,119,047	2,544,913	13,130,977	1,285,631
Corn (bushels)	20,061,049	2,157,063	73,543,190	30,776,293	38,319,999	15,065,606
Wool (bushels)	9,454,474	377,267	10,608,927	946,227	2,510,019	427,102
Pigs	910,178	73,948	2,251,653	2,036,116	1,599,919	965,779
Meat Cattle	727,837	97,201	895,077	631,707		320,209
Manufacturing						
Firearms Manufacturers	37	7	20	5	10	2
Gun Parts	0	1	0	0	0	0
Gunpowder Factory	4	3	4	0	0	1
Iron Factory	316	121	182	8	91	1
Locomotive Factories	0	5	0	0	1	0

HANDOUT 8.1, CONTINUED

	New York	Massachusetts	Ohio	Georgia	Virginia	South Carolina
Men's Clothing Factory	860	196	448	7	63	9
Military Provisions	37	3	0	0	0	0
Total Money Invested	$172,895,692	$132,792,327	$57,295,303	$10,890,875	$26,935,560	$6,931,756
Population						
Men (20–40)	624,396	202,653	350,497	85,183	225,477	42,337
Immigrants	1,001,283	260,106	328,249	11,671	35,058	9,986

Manufacturing	All Confederate States	All Union States
Firearms Manufacturers	41	189
Gun Parts	0	6
Gunpowder Factory	2	56
Iron Factory	240	1,607
Locomotives	1	18
Men's Clothing Factory	352	3,362
Military Provisions	2	13
Total Money Invested	$95,974,585	$910,132,624

LESSON 3

ORGANIZING QUESTION

What was the purpose of the "Gettysburg Address"?

STRATEGIES USED

Quick Write, Anticipation Guide

MATERIALS NEEDED

1. Online versions of the following to display for students:
    ✓ Photographs: U.S. soldiers currently serving anywhere in the world
    ✓ Photograph: *Lincoln's Gettysburg Address, Gettysburg* (1863), available at http://www.loc.gov/pictures/item/2012648250/
    ✓ Photograph: Alexander Gardner's (1863) *Dedication Ceremonies at the Soldiers' National Cemetery, Gettysburg, Pennsylvania*, available at http://www.loc.gov/pictures/resource/ppmsca.17807/

2. One copy per student of
    ✓ Speech: Lincoln's (1863) "Gettysburg Address", available at http://www.ourdocuments.gov/doc.php?doc=36&page=transcript
    ✓ Anticipation Guide: Lincoln's Gettysburg Address (**Handout 8.2**)

LESSON PLAN

Lesson Hook: *Quick Write*—On a screen, display pictures of U.S. soldiers currently serving around the world. Ask students to spend 5 minutes responding in writing to the following prompt:

> Why do members of the U.S. military deserve respect from the nation?
> If you could thank them for their service, what would you say?

Ask student volunteers to share responses and any personal connections they may have with someone serving in the military.

The Organizing Question: Explain that they will examine the text of a speech made by Abraham Lincoln on November 19, 1863, in Gettysburg, PA, to determine an answer to the organizing question: What was the purpose of the "Gettysburg Address"?

Examine the Sources: Introduce this portion of the lesson by showing *Lincoln's Gettysburg Address, Gettysburg* (1863) and Alexander Gardner's (1863) *Dedication Ceremonies at the Soldiers' National Cemetery, Gettysburg, Pennsylvania* on a screen. As you display each image, ask students these questions:

- What do you notice in this photograph?
- What do you think was happening?
- Why do you think the people were gathered at this scene?
- When do you think this picture was taken?
- What evidence from the photograph leads you to think that?

Anticipation Guide—Give each student a copy of **Handout 8.2**. Ask students to individually read the five statements and place an "X" on whether they agree or disagree. Explain to the class that they will now read the "Gettysburg Address" with a partner. While they are reading, they should look for evidence in the speech to prove or disprove their initial opinions. Partners can work together to add evidence to the second page of the anticipation guide. Circulate and help students with difficult vocabulary and content misconceptions.

Make a Hypothesis: Once students have finished reading the speech with their partners and completing the evidence section of the anticipation guide, have them answer the three reflection questions on how their opinions have changed, what their hypothesis is, and what evidence from the text helped them create that hypothesis. Allow students to share their hypotheses with class. Conclude the lesson by having students compare and contrast Lincoln's ideas with the thoughts they expressed in the lesson hook Quick Write task.

HANDOUT 8.2
ANTICIPATION GUIDE:
LINCOLN'S "GETTYSBURG ADDRESS"

PART I

Directions: Carefully read the statements below. Think about the statement and determine if you agree or disagree by marking an "X" next to your answer. Be sure to provide an explanation for your response by writing it next to the "Why?"

1. Lincoln believed that America was founded on the ideals of liberty and equality.
   ❑ Agree   ❑ Disagree
   Why? _____
   _____

2. Lincoln thought the soldiers who died might have died in vain.
   ❑ Agree   ❑ Disagree
   Why? _____
   _____

3. Lincoln valued liberty more than equality.
   ❑ Agree   ❑ Disagree
   Why? _____
   _____

4. Lincoln wanted to make ordinary citizens feel responsible for the preservation of our national ideals.
   ❑ Agree   ❑ Disagree
   Why? _____
   _____

PART II

Directions: As you read the text, cite examples of evidence that will help you agree or disagree with these statements.

1. Lincoln believed that America was founded on the ideals of liberty and equality.
   Evidence from text:
   _____
   _____
   _____
   _____

HANDOUT 8.2, CONTINUED

2. Lincoln thought that the soldiers who died might have died in vain.
   Evidence from text:

   _____

   _____

   _____

   _____

3. Lincoln valued liberty more than equality.
   Evidence from text:

   _____

   _____

   _____

   _____

4. Lincoln wanted to make ordinary citizens feel responsible for the preservation of our national ideals.
   Evidence from text:

   _____

   _____

   _____

   _____

REFLECTION QUESTIONS:

1. Did your original predictions change after reading the "Gettysburg Address"? If so, how?

   _____

   _____

   _____

2. Based on your close reading and partner discussion of the speech, what is your hypothesis to answer this question: What was the purpose of the "Gettysburg Address"?

   _____

   _____

   _____

3. What phrases from the speech are the most powerful in explaining Lincoln's purpose?

   _____

   _____

   _____

1863-1877

CHAPTER 9

RECONSTRUCTION

With malice toward none, with charity for all, with firmness in the right as God gives us to see the right, let us strive on to finish the work we are in, to bind up the nation's wounds, to care for him who shall have borne the battle and for his widow and his orphan, to do all which may achieve and cherish a just and lasting peace among ourselves and with all nations.—Abraham Lincoln's Second Inaugural Address, March 4, 1865

HISTORICAL BACKGROUND: WHAT DO I NEED TO KNOW?

The period of Reconstruction during and after the Civil War saw a great deal of change as the Union wrestled with a number of interrelated issues. Foremost was the utter destruction in the Confederate states. Major cities lay in ruins, and by the end of the war around 750,000 people on both sides of the conflict had died—about 10% of the men of fighting age. In some areas of the South, the percentage was far higher, which meant fewer men of marriageable age and fewer men to perform labor. Any program of Reconstruction would have to include a plan to rebuild the economy.

A pressing question, though, was the place of African Americans in the nation. Would they be able to vote? Were they full citizens? More than 180,000 African American men served in the Union Army by the end of the war, and they and many Whites felt that they had earned full citizenship. To this end, the United States created the Freedmen's Bureau, a government agency tasked with helping newly freed slaves find work, find lost relatives, and obtain clothing, housing, or even meals. Its crowning achievement was to help provide education to the former slaves.

A divisive problem was how to reintegrate the former Confederate States into the Union. President Lincoln, during what is called "Presidential Reconstruction," favored a moderate approach. Once 10% of a state's White population took a loyalty oath and accepted abolition, they would receive a pardon, could form a state government, and could apply for readmission to the Union. Only a few high-profile Confederates did not qualify for amnesty. President Andrew Johnson extended this plan to include a requirement that states adopt the 13th Amendment, which abolished slavery. By 1866 most former Confederate states had complied, and Johnson viewed Reconstruction as complete.

However, radical Republicans felt that the South should be punished, and in 1866 they implemented what was called Radical, or Congressional, Reconstruction. The 13th Amendment guaranteed freedom for African Americans, but many former Confederates returned to power in Southern states, and African Americans faced systematic abuses, including physical and mental abuses and denial of the right to vote. Radical Republicans believed that Southern Whites were fundamentally hostile to African Americans and that change required federal intervention.

In a first step, Radicals refused to seat incoming Southern Congressmen. They then set up a joint committee on Reconstruction. Passage of the 14th Amendment confirmed the citizenship of anyone born or naturalized in the United States and provided protections for citizens. It also, however, referred to adult "male citizens," thus sanctioning the denial of suffrage for women. Still, abuses persisted, and Radicals proposed the 15th Amendment, which declared that the right to vote could not be denied based on "race, color, or previous condition of servitude." Finally, the Military Reconstruction Act divided the former Confederate states into military districts and required stringent measures for those states to be readmitted to the Union. By the early 1870s, most Northern Whites had become tired of fighting the resistance of Southern Whites and turned to other issues of national importance.

STANDARDS ADDRESSED

NCHS U.S. History Content Standards, Grades 5–12:
- The course and character of the Civil War and its effects on the American people
- How various Reconstruction plans succeeded or failed

CCSS for Literacy in History/Social Studies, Grades 6–8:
- Integrate visual information (e.g., in charts, graphs, photographs, videos, or maps) with other information in print and digital texts.
- Determine the central ideas or information of a primary or secondary source: provide an accurate summary of the source distinct from prior knowledge or opinions.

LESSON 1

ORGANIZING QUESTION

What problems existed at the end of the Civil War?

STRATEGIES USED

Think Aloud, Gallery Walk

MATERIALS NEEDED

1. One copy per student of Reconstruction Clue Sheet (**Handout 9.1**)
2. One copy of each primary source posted in stations around the room:
   - ✓ Photograph: *Alfred Murphy, an Ex-Slave* (n.d.), available at http://dbs.ohiohistory.org/africanam/html/page857b.html?ID=4426
   - ✓ Illustrations: *Destruction of the Depots, Public Buildings, and Manufactories at Atlanta, Georgia, November 15, 1864* (1864), and *The Fourteenth and Twentieth Corps Moving out of Atlanta, November 15, 1864* (1864), available at http://www.loc.gov/pictures/item/00652832/
   - ✓ Photograph: *Ruins of Atlanta, GA, 1864* (1864), available at http://docsteach.org/documents/528865/detail
   - ✓ Photograph: *Negro Laborers at Alexandria Near Coal Wharf* (ca. 1860–1865), available at http://docsteach.org/documents/524820/detail?mode=browse&menu=closed&type%5B%5D=image&sortBy=era&page=18
   - ✓ Painting: Alexander Hay Ritchie's (ca. 1868) *Sherman's March to the Sea*, available at http://www.loc.gov/pictures/resource/ppmsca.09326/
   - ✓ Chart: Civil War Casualties (**Handout 9.2**)

LESSON PLAN

Lesson Hook: Locate pictures online of a city or country in the world that has recently been affected by a war or natural disaster. Ask students to brainstorm how they would go about rebuilding this city or country and what resources might be needed. List their ideas on the board and prompt their thinking about political, economic, and social effects of this crisis.

The Organizing Question: Explain that students will examine a variety of primary sources placed throughout the room that are clues to help them answer the organizing question: What problems existed at the end of the Civil War?

Examine the Sources: *Think Aloud*—Explain to students that they will work with a partner to collect evidence from the clues around the room and fill out the first and second columns on the Reconstruction Clue Sheet (**Handout 9.1**). Model the thinking you want students to do by displaying the image *Alfred Murphy, an Ex-Slave* (n.d.) on a document camera or screen. Using a think aloud, share your thoughts about important details from the image and questions you might have. Have the class help pick out important details by giving specific evidence from the photograph. As a class, write ideas together about what problems existed after the Civil War that this image might portray. Model how and where they should write these clues and the sources on their graphic organizer.

Gallery Walk—Next, divide the class into groups of two or three and have them walk around the room, examine each image in the clue stations, and collect evidence on their clue sheet.

Make a Hypothesis: After they have visited all clue stations, have each group write a hypothesis about what problems existed after the Civil War. As they share their hypotheses, make sure they cite evidence from the images. Let the whole class brainstorm some possible ways to solve these problems. Compare or contrast these ideas with the ideas from the lesson hook list.

HANDOUT 9.1
RECONSTRUCTION CLUE SHEET

U.S. Problems After the Civil War	Source	What Was a Solution?	Did It Work?	What Is Your Evidence?

HANDOUT 9.2
CIVIL WAR CASUALTIES

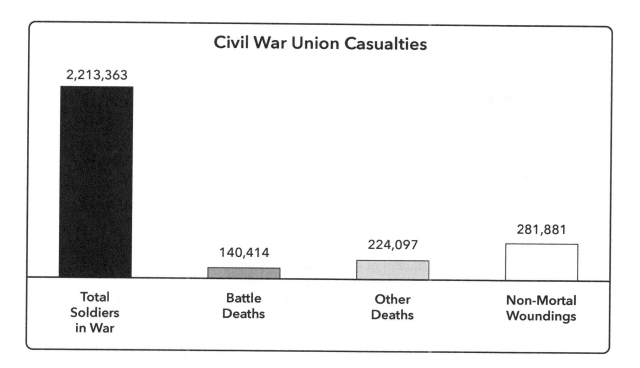

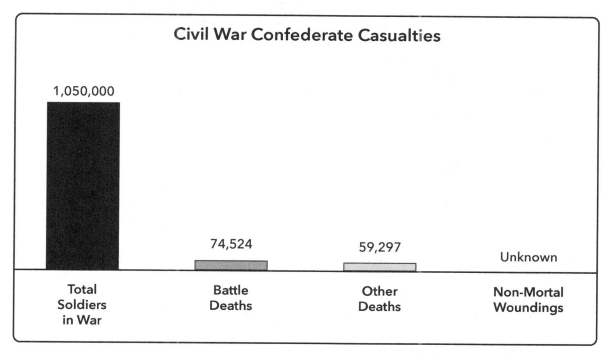

LESSON 2

ORGANIZING QUESTION

What were the competing visions for rebuilding the country?

STRATEGIES USED

Picture Prediction, Reciprocal Reading, Very Important Points (VIPs)

MATERIALS NEEDED

1. One copy per student of Reconstruction Clue Sheet (**Handout 9.1**)
2. One copy per student of each primary source:
    ✓ Political cartoon: Thomas Nast's (1864) "The Union Christmas Dinner," available at http://www.harpweek.com/09Cartoon/Browse ByDateCartoon.asp?Month=December&Date=31
    ✓ Speech: Abraham Lincoln's (1865) Second Inaugural Address, available at http://www.ourdocuments.gov/doc.php?flash=true&doc=38
    ✓ Government document: First Reconstruction Act (1867), available at http://teachingamericanhistory.org/library/index.asp?document =1920 (*Note:* We recommend using sections 1–5.)
    ✓ Speech: Excerpts From Andrew Johnson's (1867) "Veto for the First Reconstruction Act" (**Handout 9.3**; *Note:* This speech is optional in this lesson.)

LESSON PLAN

Lesson Hook: *Picture Prediction*—Display Thomas Nast's (1864) "The Union Christmas Dinner" on a screen and give students their own copy of the image. Have students respond to the image by prompting them with the following questions: What people, words, or images do you notice? What do you think Thomas Nast was trying to portray with this political cartoon? Have students write on the back of the image a prediction of what they think Lincoln's vision for Reconstruction might have been based on their evidence from the image.

The Organizing Question: Explain that students will examine some clues to help them answer the organizing question: What were the competing visions for rebuilding the country?

Examine the Sources: *Reciprocal Reading* and *Very Important Points (VIPs)*—
Organize the class into groups of three and give out copies of Excerpts From
Lincoln's (1867) "Second Inaugural Address." Divide the text into sections or
chunks, discuss the background of the speech, and explain that students' task
is to find out what Lincoln's plan for The Reconstruction was. In groups, have
students take turns reading a chunk of the speech out loud. While the first student is reading aloud, the other two students should annotate VIPs from that
section. At the end of each chunk of text, have students share what they marked
as important points and discuss any questions they have. Then switch readers
and continue the process. Make sure all three students get to read.

Explain to students that Congress also had a plan for rebuilding the country.
Introduce the First Reconstruction Act. Have students work in their reciprocal
reading groups to read and annotate the First Reconstruction Act for VIPs. If
needed, model the first paragraph and section one of this act with the class
before they begin their own reading. Remind them that they are looking for
answers to these questions: What Reconstruction plan did Congress want? How
was that similar or different to Lincoln's plan? When they have finished reading
and discussing this whole text, have them add those ideas to **Handout 9.1**.

Make a Hypothesis: When Reciprocal Reading groups are finished with discussions, have students make a hypothesis about how Lincoln's plan differed
from the plan made by Congress. Require them to cite specific evidence from
both documents as they make their arguments. As a whole class, compare and
contrast their hypotheses with ideas brainstormed from "The Union Christmas
Dinner." Add this content to **Handout 9.1**.

Optional third text: If you would like to include another primary source
to this lesson, include Excerpts From Andrew Johnson's (1867) Veto for the
Reconstruction Act (**Handout 9.3**). Have students read it together and determine how President Andrew Johnson felt about the Reconstruction Act.

HANDOUT 9.3
EXCERPTS FROM ANDREW JOHNSON'S (1867) "VETO FOR THE FIRST RECONSTRUCTION ACT"

I have examined the bill "to provide for the more efficient government of the rebel States" with the care and the anxiety which its transcendent importance is calculated to awaken. I am unable to give it my assent for reasons so grave that I hope a statement of them may have some influence on the minds of the patriotic and enlightened men with whom the decision must ultimately rest . . .

I submit to Congress whether this measure is not in its whole character, scope, and object without precedent and without authority, in palpable conflict with the plainest provisions of the Constitution, and utterly destructive to those great principles of liberty and humanity for which our ancestors on both sides of the Atlantic have shed so much blood and expended so much treasure.

The ten States named in the bill are divided into five districts. For each district an officer of the Army, not below the rank of a brigadier-general, is to be appointed to rule over the people; and he is to be supported with an efficient military force to enable him to perform his duties and enforce his authority . . .

The power thus given to the commanding officer over all the people of each district is that of an absolute monarch. His mere will is to take the place of all law. The law of the States is now the only rule applicable to the subjects placed under his control, and that is completely displaced by the clause which declares all interference of State authority to be null and void. He alone is permitted to determine what are rights of person or property, and he may protect them in such way as in his discretion may seem proper. It places at his free disposal all the lands and goods in his district, and he may distribute them without let or hindrance to whom he pleases. Being bound by no State law, and there being no other law to regulate the subject, he may make a criminal code of his own; and he can make it as bloody as any recorded in history, or he can reserve the privilege of acting upon the impulse of his private passions in each case that arises. He is bound by no rules of evidence; there is, indeed, no provision by which he is authorized or required to take any evidence at all. Everything is a crime which he chooses to call so, and all persons are condemned whom he pronounces to be guilty. He is not bound to keep and record or make any report of his proceedings. He may arrest his victims wherever he finds them, without warrant, accusation, or proof of probable cause. If he gives them a trial before he inflicts the punishment, he gives it of his grace and mercy, not because he is commanded so to do.

. . . Such a power has not been wielded by any monarch in England for more than five hundred years. In all that time no people who speak the English language have borne such servitude. It reduces the whole population of the ten States-all persons, of every color, sex, and condition, and every stranger within their limits-to the most abject and degrading slavery. No master ever had a control so absolute over the slaves as this bill gives to the military officers over both white and colored persons.

LESSON 3

ORGANIZING QUESTION

What was the immediate legacy of the Reconstruction?

STRATEGIES USED

Freewriting, Jigsaw, Position Continuum

MATERIALS NEEDED

1. Depending on class size, five or six copies of each primary source for expert group meetings:

    ✓ Document: 13th, 14th, and 15th Amendments to the U.S. Constitution, available at http://www.archives.gov/exhibits/charters /constitution_amendments_11-27.html

    ✓ Photograph: *James Plantation Freedmen's Bureau School* (ca. 1868), available at http://history.ncsu.edu/projects/cwnc/items/show/180

    ✓ Photograph: *South Carolina Government Carpenter's Shops* (n.d.), available at http://www.archives.gov/global-pages/larger-image. html?i=/research/african-americans/freedmens-bureau/images/ carpenters-shop-l.jpg&c=/research/african-americans/freedmens- bureau/images/carpenters-shop.caption.html

    ✓ Political cartoon: "The First Vote" (1867), available at http:// blackhistory.harpweek.com/7Illustrations/Reconstruction/The FirstVote.htm

    ✓ Political cartoon: Thomas Nast's (1874) "Worse than Slavery," available at http://blackhistory.harpweek.com/7Illustrations/ Reconstruction/UnionAsItWas.htm

    ✓ Interview with Emma Falconer (ca. 1930s), available at http://www. loc.gov/teachers/classroommaterials/presentationsandactivities/ presentations/timeline/civilwar/freedmen/emmafal.html

LESSON PLAN

Lesson Hook: *Freewriting*—Ask students to write a response to these questions for 5 minutes. If needed, prompt their thinking by giving either a humorous or serious personal example. Allow volunteers to share their responses.

Think of a time when you developed a plan of action. What was your plan? Did it work? What made it successful or unsuccessful?

The Organizing Question: Explain that students will examine a variety of clues (letters, pictures, and political cartoons) to form a hypothesis answering the organizing question: What was the immediate legacy of Reconstruction?

Examine the Sources: Begin the lesson by having students review various Reconstruction plans to solve the problems facing the United States after the Civil War.

Jigsaw—Divide the class into groups with six students in each. These groups will be the home groups. First, have each group brainstorm their initial thoughts on the meaning of the word *legacy* and discuss these as a whole class. Each group should assign all six members a letter from A–F. Those letter groups will become experts on a certain "clue" to help answer the organizing question. Have six "expert" stations around the room with a copy of each source posted:

- Station A: 13th, 14th, and 15th Amendments to the U.S. Constitution
- Station B: *James Plantation Freedmen's Bureau School* (ca. 1868)
- Station C: *South Carolina Government Carpenter's Shops* (n.d.)
- Station D: "The First Vote" (n.d.)
- Station E: "Worse than Slavery"
- Station F: Interview with Emma Falconer (ca. 1930s)

Students should go to an assigned station with their letter or expert group. As an expert group, have them decide how that source helps answer the organizing question. Use the following questions to prompt student thinking:

- What is the main idea of your source?
- How do you know that?
- Is it positive or negative evidence?

Have students return to home groups and explain the source to the other students. In their home groups, have students use their evidence to complete **Handout 9.1**.

Make a Hypothesis: *Position Continuum*—As a culminating formative assessment, have students individually write whether or not Reconstruction was successful based on the evidence they examined. Once they finish writing, have them create a Position Continuum along the wall of the room (Strongly Agree, Agree, Disagree, Strongly Disagree). Students should stand at a spot along the line based on their hypothesis about the legacy of Reconstruction. Once they are in place, ask students to explain why they are standing in that position using evidence from the lesson sources.

1840-1914

CHAPTER 10

A NATION IN TRANSITION

We must onward to the fulfillment of our mission—to the entire development of the principle of our organization—freedom of conscience, freedom of person, freedom of trade and business pursuits, universality of freedom and equality. This is our high destiny, and in nature's eternal, inevitable decree of cause and effect we must accomplish it.—John L. O'Sullivan, "The Great Nation of Futurity," 1839

HISTORICAL BACKGROUND: WHAT DO I NEED TO KNOW?

For several hundred years the promise of easy access to open land served as a central feature of the American experience. Over the course of the 19th century, the mean center of population in the United States moved from just east of Baltimore, MD, in 1790, to just west of Bloomington, IN, on the eve of World War I. In 1845 newspaperman John O'Sullivan coined the term "Manifest Destiny" to describe the feeling that the American experience was morally superior and that Americans had an obligation to spread these ideas, nonviolently, to people around the world.

The American West became a focus of this ideal as settlers poured onto the plains in ever-increasing numbers. Gold in California, silver in Nevada, copper in Colorado, various precious minerals elsewhere, and a seemingly endless stretch of rich farmland lured settlers from Europe out West. Native American nations, many of whom did not get along with each other and could not effectively fight the tide of incomers, in turn accommodated, fought against, and tried to divert settlers. The onrush was too great.

Americans after the midcentury were relieved that the nation had survived the great test of the Civil War, and that Reconstruction, even if not concluded to the satisfaction of many Northern Whites, had at least brought the former Confederate states back into the union. For the United States, the 1876 World's Fair in Philadelphia featured a look back at the first hundred years of American history. One exhibit featured a colonial kitchen while another celebrated the trials and tribulations of the Revolutionary War. Artwork highlighted settlement of the American West. The message of these exhibits was that despite the devastation of the Civil War, Americans could take pride in how far the United States had progressed in the century since 1776.

The World's Fair was also a chance to showcase manufacturing, agriculture, and progress, including curiosities such as the telephone, typewriters, Heinz Ketchup, root beer, and the arm for the Statue of Liberty. For Europeans who thought of the United States as a backward nation beset by civil war and the political scandals of the late 1860s and early 1870s, the fair announced the United States as a soon-to-be world power.

The entrance of the United States onto the world stage came at a time when European powers held long-established colonies around the world. The United States would therefore try to encourage rebellion in the colonies of weaker world powers or make outright war in order to take them. The United States had long eyed Cuba, and the end of the Civil War brought renewed interest in the island, and in all of the Caribbean, Central America, and South America. A series of Cuban wars for independence beginning in 1868 saw some U.S. support. Then in 1898, the armored cruiser *USS Maine* exploded and sank in the Havana Harbor. Newspapers eager to expand circulation fanned the flames of war, and pro-imperialist politicians seized the opportunity. In the 1898 Spanish-American War, the United States captured Spanish holdings including Cuba and the Philippines, signaling that the U.S. had joined European nations as an imperial power.

Many Americans celebrated that expansion of power. In what by modern standards would be horribly racist depictions, political cartoonists applauded the introduction of American ideals to "backward" peoples. Others, mindful of the philosophy of the Declaration of Independence and the just-passed centennial celebrations, questioned whether dominance over colonial possessions signaled a fundamental hypocrisy in American international politics.

STANDARDS ADDRESSED

NCHS U.S. History Content Standards, Grades 5–12:

- United States territorial expansion between 1801 and 1861, and how it affected relations with external powers and Native Americans
- How the industrial revolution, increasing immigration, the rapid expansion of slavery, and the westward movement changed the lives of Americans and led toward regional tensions

CCSS for Literacy in History/Social Studies, Grades 6–8:

- Cite specific textual evidence to support analysis of primary and secondary sources.
- Identify aspects of a text that reveal an author's point of view or purposes (e.g., loaded language, inclusion or avoidance of particular facts).
- Integrate visual information (e.g., in charts, graphs, photographs, videos, or maps) with other information in print and digital texts.

LESSON 1

ORGANIZING QUESTION
What viewpoints about Westward expansion were portrayed in American art?

STRATEGIES USED
Brainstorming With Visuals, Analyzing Photographs and Prints

MATERIALS NEEDED
1. An online copy of John Gast's (1872) *American Progress*
2. One copy per student of the Library of Congress Analyzing Photographs and Prints Template, available at http://www.loc.gov/teachers/using primarysources/resources/Analyzing_Photographs_and_Prints.pdf
3. Three or four copies for each group of one of the following sources:
   ✓ Mural: Emanuel Leutze's (1862) *Westward the Course of Empire Takes its Way*, available at http://www.aoc.gov/capitol-hill/other-paintings-and-murals/westward-course-empire-takes-its-way
   ✓ Illustration: Theodore Davis's (1869) *Pilgrims on the Plains*, available at http://thewest.harpweek.com/Illustrations/!ListOfIllusHeader.htm
   ✓ Illustration: Albert Bierstadt's (1859) *Crossing the Platte*, available at http://thewest.harpweek.com/Illustrations/!ListOfIllusHeader.htm
   ✓ Painting: Albert Bierstadt's (1868) *Among the Sierra Nevada, California*, available at http://americanart.si.edu/t2go/1lw/index-noframe.html?/t2go/1lw/lw-index.html
   ✓ Print: Fanny Palmer's (ca. 1868) *Across the Continent: Westward the Course of Empire Takes its Way*, available at http://www.loc.gov/pictures/resource/cph.3f03757/

4. A blank sheet of white paper and a few markers or colored pencils per student

LESSON PLAN

Lesson Hook: *Brainstorming With Visuals*—As students enter class, have them pick up a blank piece of paper and two or three colored pencils. Give students 5–10 minutes to draw pictures of what images come to mind when they think of the West. Allow students to share their visuals. Ask them where they think the ideas came from and whether or not they might be accurate.

The Organizing Question: Explain that students will look at several images about Westward expansion to answer the organizing question: What viewpoints about Westward expansion were portrayed in American art?

Examine the Sources: *Analyzing Photographs and Prints*—Display John Gast's (1872) *American Progress* on a screen and give each student a copy of the Analyzing Photographs and Prints template. Model with students how to respond to the questions in the Observe, Reflect, and Question sections of the template as they analyze different parts of the painting. End the discussion with these questions:

- What perspectives on Westward expansion were represented?
- Are there any perspectives missing?
- What was the artist's point of view on Westward expansion?
- How do you know that from the painting?

Divide the class into five groups and give each group copies of a work of art about the West. Explain to students that they will work with their group members to analyze the artwork using the same template questions: Reflect, Observe, and Question. As they finish their analyses, challenge them to be able to present to the whole class answers to the four questions above.

Make a Hypothesis: Show the electronic color versions of the image on a screen while the groups display their images and what they think it means. When each group is finished, have students use all of the images to make a hypothesis about the organizing question. They may do this individually or with their groups. Ask students what other information they might need to know to accurately and thoroughly respond to the question.

Next, have them go back to their pictures from the lesson hook portion and see what content might be missing. An idea for a summative assessment could be for students to draw their own version of Gast's (1872) *American Progress* after they have studied the content from this unit.

LESSON 2

ORGANIZING QUESTION

How did Americans in 1876 view changes over the previous 100 years?

STRATEGIES USED

Picture Prediction, Analyzing Prints

MATERIALS NEEDED

1. Online version of Currier and Ives's (ca. 1876) *The Stride of a Century*, http://www.loc.gov/pictures/item/93506699/
2. One copy of these sources for half of the class, printed in color if possible (If you can print and laminate a classroom set, they can be used again. Students can then use dry erase markers to circle clues.)
   ✓ Print: *Centennial Mirror* (n.d.), available at http://www.loc.gov/pictures/resource/cph.3b52134/
   ✓ Print: Henry Schile's (1876) *1776, Centennial International Exhibition, 1876, History of the United States*, available at http://www.loc.gov/pictures/item/2003656440/

3. One copy per student of the Library of Congress Analyzing Photographs and Prints template, available at http://www.loc.gov/teachers/using primarysources/resources/Analyzing_Photographs_and_Prints.pdf4. Optional: Chart paper and markers or art supplies for each group (for lesson extension only)
4. Optional: Ten to fifteen magnifying glasses to use to examine the image (These are available at teacher supply stores or dollar stores.)

LESSON PLAN

Lesson Hook: *Picture Prediction*—Begin class by having Currier and Ives's (ca. 1876) *The Stride of a Century* displayed on a screen. Ask students to write down all of the people, places, dates, and words they notice in the image. Then have them predict what they think the image might mean. Allow several students to share their thoughts. Have them hold these predictions to re-examine at the end of the lesson.

The Organizing Question: Explain that students will examine two images to find evidence or clues to answer the organizing question: How did Americans in 1876 view changes over the previous 100 years?

Examine the Sources: *Analyzing Prints*—Give half of the class a copy of *Centennial Mirror* (n.d.) and the other half Schile's (1876) *1776, Centennial International Exhibition, 1876, History of the United States.* Explain why both images were created and briefly ask students to brainstorm what historical events took place during that 100-year period in U.S. history. Give each student a copy of the Analyzing Photographs and Prints template. If you have magnifying glasses, pass those out so students can see the details in the images.

Have students answer the questions on the Analyzing Photographs and Prints handout about their assigned side of the painting with a partner who also has the same image. Once they have discussed the answers to the questions with their partner, have students circle (if laminated) or write down a list of clues from the image that might help answer the organizing question.

Now pair students who analyzed different prints together. Have students share their clues about how Americans viewed changes throughout the century. Circulate and clarify any misconceptions students may have. Prompt students to locate details in each image and compare and contrast the two. Ask them to think about why the artists chose to include certain inventions, events, or scenes.

Make a Hypothesis: Once students have finished sharing their evidence from the two images, ask them to write a hypothesis statement that answers the organizing question. Allow students to share their hypotheses with supporting evidence from both images as you display larger versions of the images on a screen. When all of the students have shared their hypotheses, return to Currier and Ives's (1876) *The Stride of a Century*. Ask them to give their interpretations of its meaning based on the two prints they examined in class.

Optional lesson extension: Allow students to choose another century before or after 1876 (1576, 1676, 1976, or 2076) and design a painting similar to the two examined in the lesson that either reflects the changes from that particular time period or predicts what they may be in the future. Have students use a format similar to either image and create them on chart paper with markers or other art supplies.

LESSON 3

ORGANIZING QUESTION
How did political cartoons help justify American imperialism?

STRATEGIES USED
Analyzing Political Cartoons, Gallery Walk

MATERIALS NEEDED
1. An online version of Louis Dalrymple's (1899) "School Begins" to show during the lesson hook, available at http://www.loc.gov/pictures/resource/ppmsca.28668/
2. One or two copies of each of the following sources, placed on the wall or in stations around the room:
    ✓ Political cartoon: Philadelphia Press's (1898) "Ten Thousand Miles from Tip to Tip," available at http://commons.wikimedia.org/wiki/File:10kMiles.JPG
    ✓ Political cartoon: John T. McCutcheon's (1914) "What the United States has Fought For," available from https://upload.wikimedia.org/wikipedia/commons/e/e4/Free_from_Spanish.jpg
    ✓ Political cartoon: Louis Dalrymple's (1905) "The World's Constable," available at http://www.loc.gov/pictures/resource/ds.05213/
    ✓ Political cartoon: Charles Bartholomew's (1898) "Will Wear the Stars and Stripes," available at http://history.house.gov/Exhibitions-and-Publications/HAIC/Historical-Essays/Foreign-Domestic/Legislative-Interests/
    ✓ Political cartoon: J. S. Pughe's (1900) "Hurrah! The Country is Saved Again!," available at http://www.loc.gov/pictures/resource/ppmsca.25473/

3. One copy per student of the Imperialism Graphic Organizer (**Handout 10.1**)

LESSON PLAN
(*Note:* This lesson works best after students have a basic understanding of U.S. imperialism and the countries and presidents involved.)

Lesson Hook: *Analyzing a Political Cartoon*—Begin class by displaying "School Begins" (Dalrymple, 1899) on a screen. Tell students they are going to be detectives and try to figure out what the image means by examining clues in the cartoon. Ask them the following questions about the cartoon and prompt their thinking as they examine the many people and words throughout this cartoon:

- What people, objects, or symbols do you see in the cartoon?
- What seems to be happening in the scene?
- What words or dates do you see in the cartoon?
- What do you think the cartoonist was trying to say about imperialism?
- Why do you think that?
- What questions do you have about this cartoon?

The Organizing Question: Explain that students will examine several political cartoons around the room to try to answer the organizing question: How did political cartoons help justify American imperialism?

Examine the Sources: *Gallery Walk*—Tell students that they are going to use their detective skills developed in the lesson hook segment to examine five political cartoons and try to use the clues to figure out the meaning. Divide students into groups of three and give them a copy of **Handout 10.1**. Have them complete the graphic organizer while analyzing the political cartoons around the room.

Make a Hypothesis: In their groups, have students complete the reflection question about noticing similarities and patterns. Once they generate their similarities list, have them develop a hypothesis with supporting evidence to answer the organizing question. Allow groups to share their hypotheses and evidence from all five political cartoons. Display online versions of the cartoons while students share what they noticed and the cartoonists' messages. To conclude, ask them to compare and contrast the five Gallery Walk cartoons with Dalrymple's (1899) "School Begins" from the lesson hook. An optional extension for this lesson is to have students create their own political cartoon that either justifies imperialism or takes a position against it.

HANDOUT 10.1
IMPERIALISM GRAPHIC ORGANIZER

Organizing Question: How did political cartoons help justify American imperialism?

Political Cartoon	What people, objects, or symbols do you see in the cartoon? What seems to be happening in the scene?	What words or dates do you see in the cartoon?	What do you think the cartoonist is trying to say about imperialism? Why do you think that?	What questions do you have about this cartoon?
"Ten Thousand Miles from Tip to Tip"				
"What the U.S. Has Fought For"				
"The World's Constable"				
"Will Wear the Stars and Stripes"				
"Hurrah! The Country is Saved Again"				

HANDOUT 10.1, CONTINUED

1. What similarities or patterns did you notice in the five cartoons?

    _____

    _____

    _____

    _____

    _____

    _____

    _____

    _____

2. My hypothesis is:

    _____

    _____

    _____

    _____

    _____

    _____

    _____

3. The evidence to support my hypothesis is:

    _____

    _____

    _____

    _____

    _____

    _____

    _____

1840-1900

CHAPTER 11

INDUSTRIALIZATION AND IMMIGRATION

Long ago it was said that "one half of the world does not know how the other half lives." That was true then. It did not know because it did not care. The half that was on top cared little for the struggles, and less for the fate of those who were underneath, so long as it was able to hold them there and keep its own seat. There came a time when the discomfort and crowding below were so great, and the consequent upheavals so violent, that it was no longer an easy thing to do, and then the upper half fell to inquiring what was the matter.—Jacob Riis, *How the Other Half Lives: Studies Among the Tenements of New York*, 1890

HISTORICAL BACKGROUND: WHAT DO I NEED TO KNOW?

Even as Westward movement continued to define Americans' understandings of themselves, the nation was changing. In 1870, for the first time, fewer than half of all employed people were farmers, and in 1890 the U.S. Census Bureau announced that there was no longer any real frontier in the United States—all the land had been settled an explored.

The United States was becoming an industrialized nation and needed all the labor it could attract. Industry first took hold in population-dense New England in the early 19th century. The numerous ports provided easy access to international markets as well as a place for immigrants to land. In the 1820s the textile industry held great promise, early mills employed farm girls drawn by steady cash income and the assurance to their parents that the girls' morals would be strictly protected. They lived in mill towns under the rule of pious matrons. One group, the Lowell Mill Girls, became world famous for their independence and culture.

As the century progressed and industry expanded, factories attracted immigrant men from outside of England. Germans and Irish, historically looked down upon by the British, began to arrive in the 1820s. Their strange customs and foreign languages alarmed some Americans, but the nation was vast, and although some worked in factories, many of them moved West in search of farmland. Later in the century a new group of darker skinned immigrants who spoke little, if any, English began to arrive from Southern and Eastern Europe.

By the late 19th century most White, Western Europeans had adapted theories of natural selection to concepts of race, social science, and even national success. They understood the world to consist of a hierarchy of types, with White Europeans at the top, and a ladder of peoples descending to the bottom. Couched in quasi-scientific language, the ladder reflected pre-existing stereotypes about people with darker skin, non-Christians, and non-English speakers. Newspapers and artwork such as political cartoons portrayed the so-called lower races, such as the Irish, Eastern Europeans, and Africans, in racist caricatures.

As the number of farms dwindled and manufacturing work continued to expand in the cities, these new immigrants concentrated in tenement houses in cities divided into ethnic enclaves. Dirty, dark, and poorly ventilated tenements sometimes housed a dozen people. One 1894 survey found New York City as the most densely populated city in the world with more than 800 people per acre in some areas. Economic abuse of immigrant tenants was rampant, and the poorly constructed buildings were prone to fire, collapse, and the spread of disease.

Middle-class reformers set out to clean the cities by imposing middle-class sensibilities on the sometimes unwilling poor. Progressives, as they were known, sought to clean up and regulate everything from city water to milk to poorly labeled and uninspected food. Others, such as Jacob Riis and Lewis Hine, documented the poverty through photographs and essays. Many Progressives focused on children who, in an era before labor laws, worked in factories under often terrible conditions. Other children roamed the street, engaging in games, petty crime, or simply scrounging for food.

As the 20th century opened, many Americans looked inside the United States and saw a nation much different than the one that had entered the Civil

War. They also looked outside the borders and saw a world in which the old European rivalries they had largely avoided loomed ever more dangerously on the horizon.

STANDARDS ADDRESSED

NCHS U.S. History Content Standards, Grades 5–12:

- How the rise of corporations, heavy industry, and mechanized farming transformed the American people
- Massive immigration after 1870 and how new social patterns, conflicts, and ideas of national unity developed amid growing cultural diversity
- The rise of the American labor movement and how political issues reflected social and economic changes

CCSS for Literacy in History/Social Studies, Grades 6–8:

- Integrate visual information (e.g., in charts, graphs, photographs, videos, or maps) with other information in print and digital texts.
- Cite textual evidence to support analysis of primary and secondary sources.

LESSON 1

ORGANIZING QUESTION
What was life like for the Lowell Mill Girls?

STRATEGIES USED
Brainstorming, Mystery

MATERIALS NEEDED
1. Photograph: *Boott Mills 1890s Employees* (n.d.), available at http://libweb.uml.edu/clh/All/mi07.htm
2. One copy per student of Clue Sheet: What Was Life Like for the Lowell Mill Girls? (**Handout 11.1**)
3. Two or three copies of each of these sources, placed in eight stations around the room:
    ✓ Sketch: Winslow Homer's (n.d.) *Bobbin Girl*, available at http://libweb.uml.edu/clh/All/mgi04.htm
    ✓ Photograph: *Girl at Loom* (n.d.), available at http://libweb.uml.edu/clh/All/mgi01.htm
    ✓ Sketch: *Spinning Frame With Young Woman* (n.d.), available at http://libweb.uml.edu/clh/All/mgi02.htm
    ✓ Sketch: *Lowell Carpet Mills* (1850), available at http://libweb.uml.edu/clh/All/mi10.htm
    ✓ Letter: Sarah Rice (1845) to her father, available at http://libweb.uml.edu/clh/All/ric03.htm
    ✓ Letter: Amy Melenda Galusha (1849) to her brother, available at http://libweb.uml.edu/clh/All/gal01.htm
    ✓ Letter: Lydia Bixby (1852) to her mother, available at http://libweb.uml.edu/clh/All/bix1.htm
    ✓ Time Table: *Time Table of the Lowell Mills* (1851), available at http://libweb.uml.edu/clh/All/doc02.htm

4. Chart paper and markers

LESSON PLAN

Lesson Hook: *Brainstorming*—Explain that students will participate in three quick brainstorming sessions and should be ready to write each of the lists in their notes. Give them one minute to brainstorm answers to each of these questions:

- What are some reasons you might want or need to get a job as a teenager?
- What are some interesting jobs that teenagers can do?
- What are some possible challenges to those jobs?

Allow students to discuss their responses and pros and cons of different jobs available for teenagers in your community.

The Organizing Question: Explain that students will play the role of detectives and examine clues to answer the organizing question: What was life like for the Lowell Mill Girls?

Examine the Sources: *Mystery*—Give students copies of **Handout 11.1** and display the *Boott Mills 1890s Employees* (n.d.) photograph on a screen. Ask students to describe what they notice from the photograph and how it might be a clue to answer the question. Model for students how to write the evidence on the clue sheet.

Next, divide the class into seven detective teams and explain that there are seven stations around the room with clues to help them answer the question. Have them each pick one station and begin. The letters will take some time for students to read, so allow them to go in any order around the room, choosing stations as they become available. As teams examine a source, have them write details on their clue sheet.

Make a Hypothesis: Once teams have finished analyzing all of the clues, have them return to their seats and stay with their team. Ask them to discuss this question before they begin creating a hypothesis:

Where did you see similar ideas or overlaps between what you read in the letters and saw in the images?

Teams should then use their data to create a hypothesis that answers the question. Give each group a piece of chart paper and some markers. As a team, they should agree on a hypothesis and write it on the paper. To prove their hypothesis, have them also draw five images that demonstrate specific words or phrases from the clues. Have each group report its hypothesis and explain the visuals.

Ask students to compare and contrast the hypotheses that were created, how they think the detective task is similar to what historians do, and how the jobs of the Lowell Mill Girls might be similar to or different from the jobs of teenagers they brainstormed in the lesson hook. If time permits, have students respond in writing to these questions as a formative assessment:

- What are four details about life in the Lowell mill towns that you learned from this project?
- How was your hypothesis supported by the evidence or clues?
- How do you think this activity was similar to the job of a real historian?

HANDOUT 11.1
CLUE SHEET: WHAT WAS LIFE LIKE
FOR THE LOWELL MILL GIRLS?

As you visit the stations around the room, examine the sources and collect information to answer the organizing question. Write down important details from each source. **Examples of evidence:** How the mills operated, working conditions, type of work done, living conditions, etc.

Clues	Details
1. Photograph: Boott Mills, 1890s	
2. Time Table of the Lowell Mills	
3. Letter from Lydia Bixby	
4. Letter from Sarah Rice	
5. Letter from Amy Melenda Galusha	
6. Sketch: *Bobbin Girl*	
7. Photograph: *Girl at Loom*	
8. Sketch: *Spinning Frame With Young Woman*	

Before you make your hypothesis, discuss this question with your group: Where did you see similar ideas or overlaps between what you read in the letters and in the images?

Our Hypothesis:

_____

_____

_____

Our Best Evidence:

_____

_____

_____

LESSON 2

ORGANIZING QUESTION
How do cartoons reflect newspaper views of immigration?

STRATEGIES USED
Analyzing Political Cartoons, Modified Jigsaw

MATERIALS NEEDED
1. Choose two or three political cartoons from *U.S. News and World Report*'s website on current immigration issues: http://www.usnews.com/cartoons/immigration-cartoons
2. One copy per student of the Library of Congress's Analyzing Political Cartoons Guide, available at http://www.loc.gov/teachers/usingprimarysources/resources/Analyzing_Political_Cartoons.pdf
3. Six or seven copies of each of these cartoons for each expert group:
   - ✓ Political cartoon: Thomas Nast's (1869) "Uncle Sam's Thanksgiving Dinner," available at http://www.harpweek.com/09Cartoon/BrowseByDateCartoon.asp?Month=November&Date=22
   - ✓ Political cartoon: Thomas Nast's (1871) "The Chinese Question," available at http://www.harpweek.com/09Cartoon/BrowseByDateCartoon.asp?Month=February&Date=18
   - ✓ Political cartoon: William Rogers's (1883) "The Balance of Trade with Great Britain Seems to Still Be Against Us," available at http://www.harpweek.com/09Cartoon/BrowseByDateCartoon.asp?Month=April&Date=28
   - ✓ Political cartoon: Michael Angelo Wolfe's (1877) "Untitled," available at http://www.harpweek.com/09Cartoon/BrowseByDateCartoon.asp?Month=July&Date=28

4. One piece of white copy paper and markers for each student

LESSON PLAN

Lesson Hook: Ask students to brainstorm a list of current student issues or concerns in their school. Once they have made a list, have them choose one issue about which they have a strong opinion. Give students blank paper and markers and tell them they have 10 minutes to take a position on this issue and illustrate their position in a visual. Have students share their visuals and discuss similarities and differences in the way students represented their points of view on school issues.

The Organizing Question: Explain that students will examine 19th-century political cartoons to answer the organizing question: How do cartoons reflect newspapers' views of immigration?

Examine the Sources: *Analyzing Political Cartoons*—Locate two or three recent political cartoons on the topic of immigration from the *U.S. News and World Report* website. Display the images on a screen and give students a copy of the Library of Congress's Analyzing Political Cartoons Guide. As a whole class, guide students to respond to the questions in the Observe, Reflect, and Question sections of the guide. Make sure to focus on the cartoonists' opinions on the immigration issue and what methods were used to persuade the audience.

Modified Jigsaw—Now explain that students will examine some political cartoons from the 19th century using the same analysis guide.

Expert groups: Divide the class into four expert groups (numbered 1, 2, 3, 4, etc.) and give each group copies of one political cartoon. Explain that they will be experts on their cartoon. As an expert group, they should think about the questions from the Analyzing Political Cartoons Guide about their specific cartoon. Remind students to look at words and symbols to help determine each cartoonist's point of view on immigration. Because period political cartoons are often difficult to understand, be ready to provide either copies of the text explanation or website links for students to read about the cartoon if needed. The *Harper's Weekly* website has detailed information on each cartoon.

Home groups: Once students have finished completing the analysis in their expert groups, assign students in each group a letter such as A, B, C, and so on. Ask them to join with students who have the same letters to create a home group. Once students rearrange into home groups, there should be an expert on each political cartoon. Each expert should share the cartoon, explain the meaning, and analyze the author's purpose for other members of the home group.

Make a Hypothesis: When all students are finished with the cartoon explanations, have the home groups use all four cartoons to make a hypothesis answering the organizing question. Have one student in each home group write the group's hypothesis and supporting evidence on a paper to turn in with all group members' names included. Allow each group to share its hypothesis with evidence. Discuss the similarities and differences in their hypotheses and relate the 19th-century cartoons and themes to the current immigration cartoons.

LESSON 3

ORGANIZING QUESTION

What was life like for a child living in a city at the turn of the century?

STRATEGIES USED

Picture Prediction, Gallery Walk, Annotation

MATERIALS NEEDED

1. An online version of these images to display for students:
   - ✓ Political cartoon: "The Road to Dividends" (ca. 1913), http://www.loc.gov/pictures/resource/nclc.02853/
   - ✓ Photograph: Lewis Hine's (1908a) *Glass works. Midnight. Indiana,* available at http://www.loc.gov/pictures/resource/nclc.01151/
   - ✓ Photograph: Lewis Hine's (1908f) *Lincoln Cotton Mill, Evansville, Ind. Girl at Slubber,* available at http://www.loc.gov/pictures/resource/nclc.01330/

2. One copy of each of the following Gallery Walk photographs, posted around the room in stations with a blank piece of chart paper beside each one:
   - ✓ Lewis Hine's (1908b) *Blower and Mold Boy, Seneca Glass Works, Morgantown, W. Va,* available at http://www.loc.gov/pictures/resource/nclc.01185/?co=nclc
   - ✓ Lewis Hine's (1908g), *Mannington Glass Works,* available at http://www.loc.gov/pictures/resource/nclc.01190/
   - ✓ Lewis Hine's (1908e) *Drivers and Trappers Going Home: Barnesville Mine,* available at http://www.loc.gov/pictures/item/ncl2004000212/PP/
   - ✓ Lewis Hine's (1908d) *Citizens' Glass Co., Evansville, Ind.,* available at http://www.loc.gov/pictures/resource/nclc.01204/
   - ✓ Lewis Hine's (1908h) *Girls running warping machines in Loray mill, Gastonia, N.C.,* available at http://www.loc.gov/pictures/resource/nclc.01342/
   - ✓ Lewis Hine's (1908c) *"Carrying in Boy" at the Lehr. Glass Factory, Grafton, W. Va.,* available at http://www.loc.gov/pictures/resource/nclc.01177/

3. Chart paper and markers for Gallery Walk
4. Post-it notes for the Picture Prediction strategy
5. Copies of excerpts from Jacob Riis's (1890) *How the Other Half Lives*:
   ✓ Half of the students will receive Chapter 15 Excerpts: "The Problem with the Children" (**Handout 11.2**)
   ✓ The other half of the students will receive Chapter 20 Excerpts: "The Working Girls of New York" (**Handout 11.3**), http://ebooks. gutenberg.us/WorldeBookLibrary.com/otherhalf.htm

LESSON PLAN

Lesson Hook: *Picture Prediction*—Display "The Road to Dividends" (ca. 1913) on a screen. Give every student a Post-it note and have them answer these questions about the cartoon:
- Describe the images you notice in this political cartoon.
- What do you think the caption means?
- Based on this image, predict what you think will be the focus of today's lesson.

Allow students to share responses and have them put the Post-it note on the right corner of their desk. At the end of the lesson, they will return to this prediction.

The Organizing Question: Explain that students will examine a variety of images and written texts to find clues to answer the organizing question: What was life like for a child living in a city at the turn of the century?

Examine the Sources: *Gallery Walk*—Display Lewis Hine's (1908) *Glass works. Midnight. Indiana* on a screen for students to examine. Provide students with some background on Lewis Hine and his collection of photographs. Ask students the following questions and model your thinking about the image:
- What do you notice in the photograph?
- What questions do you have?
- How might this image help answer the organizing question?

Practice analyzing one more image by showing Hine's (1908) *Lincoln Cotton Mill, Evansville, Ind. Girl at Slubber* and discussing the same questions. Explain to students that they will work with a partner to examine the photographs around the room. As they analyze each photo, have them write their responses to the three questions on the chart paper beside each image. Allow students time to move around the room, examining the photographs at stations. When they return to their desks, have them work with their partner to generate a list of responses to the organizing question, using specific photographs as evidence. Have them share the questions they wrote on their posters as a prereading activity. Encourage them to read for answers to those questions.

Annotation—Next, explain to students that they will read excerpts from Jacob Riis's (1890) *How the Other Half Lives* to find more clues to help answer the question and understand the photos. Provide background information about Riis and the purpose of his book. Combine partner groups to create groups of four and then distribute **Handout 11.2** to one half of the class and **Handout 11.3** to the other half. Have students take turns reading sections of the text, annotating the text for clues about what life was like for children. At the end of the text discussion, have the groups write a summary at the bottom of the page of what clues they learned from their chapter excerpts. Next, regroup students who read **Handout 11.2** with students who read **Handout 11.3** and have them share summaries and evidence from the text.

Make a Hypothesis: With their new partners, ask students to take their Post-it note from the lesson hook, turn it over, and together create a hypothesis that answers the organizing question. Challenge students to use evidence from both the photographs and the written text. After students have created and shared their hypotheses and evidence, display "The Road to Dividends" (ca. 1913) on the screen again. Have students examine their prediction from the beginning and evaluate how accurate they were with interpreting the cartoon. Ask students to share evidence from the sources that helps them to further understand the meaning of the political cartoon.

HANDOUT 11.2
CHAPTER 15 EXCERPTS:
"THE PROBLEM WITH THE CHILDREN"

THE problem of the children becomes, in these swarms, to the last degree perplexing. Their very number makes one stand aghast. I have already given instances of the packing of the child population in East Side tenements. They might be continued indefinitely until the array would be enough to startle any community. For, be it remembered, these children with the training they receive—or do not receive—with the instincts they inherit and absorb in their growing up, are to be our future rulers, if our theory of government is worth anything. More than a working majority of our voters now register from the tenements. I counted the other day the little ones, up to ten years or so, in a Bayard Street tenement that for a yard has a triangular space in the center with sides fourteen or fifteen feet long, just room enough for a row of ill-smelling closets at the base of the triangle and a hydrant at the apex. There was about as much light in this "yard" as in the average cellar. I gave up my self-imposed task in despair when I had counted one hundred and twenty-eight in forty families. Thirteen I had missed, or not found in. Applying the average for the forty to the whole fifty-three, the house contained one hundred and seventy children. It is not the only time I have had to give up such census work. I have in mind an alley—an inlet rather to a row of rear tenements— that is either two or four feet wide according as the wall of the crazy old building that gives on it bulges out or in. I tried to count the children that swarmed there, but could not. Sometimes I have doubted that anybody knows just how many there are about. Bodies of drowned children turn up in the rivers right along sin summer whom no one seems to know anything about.

The old question, what to do with the boy, assumes a new and serious phase in the tenements. Under the best conditions found there, it is not easily answered. In nine cases out of ten he would make an excellent mechanic, if trained early to work at a trade, for he is neither dull nor slow, but the short-sighted despotism of the trades unions has practically closed that avenue to him. Trade-schools, however excellent, cannot supply the opportunity thus denied him, and at the outset the boy stands condemned by his own to low and ill-paid drudgery, held down by the hand that of all should labor to raise him. Home, the greatest factor of all in the training of the young, means nothing to him but a pigeon-hole in a coop along with so many other human animals. Its influence is scarcely of the elevating kind, if it have any. The very games at which he takes a hand in the street become polluting in its atmosphere. With no steady hand to guide him, the boy takes naturally to idle ways. Caught in the street by the truant officer, or by the agents of the Children's Societies, peddling, perhaps, or begging, to help out the family resources; he runs the risk of being sent to a reformatory, where contact with vicious boys older than himself soon develop the latent possibilities for evil that lie hidden in him.

A little fellow who seemed clad in but a single rag was among the flotsam and jetsam stranded at Police Headquarters one day last summer. No one knew where he came from or where he belonged. The boy himself knew as little about it as anybody, and was the least anxious to have light shed on the subject after he had spent a night in the

HANDOUT 11.2, CONTINUED

matron's nursery. The discovery that beds were provided for boys to sleep in there, and that he could have "a whole egg" and three slices of bread for breakfast put him on the best of terms with the world in general, and he decided that Headquarters was "a bully place." He sang "McGinty" all through, with Tenth Avenue variations, for the police, and then settled down to the serious business of giving an account of himself. The examination went on after this fashion:

"Where do you go to church, my boy?"

"We don't have no clothes to go to church." And indeed his appearance, as he was, in the door of any New York church would have caused a sensation.

"Well, where do you go to school, then?"

"I don't go to school," with a snort of contempt.

"Where do you buy your bread?"

"We don't buy no bread; we buy beer," said the boy, and it was eventually the saloon that led the police as a landmark to his "home." It was worthy of the boy. As he had said, his only bed was a heap of dirty straw on the floor, his daily diet a crust in the morning, nothing else.

Into the rooms of the Children's Aid Society were led two little girls whose father had "busted up the house" and put them on the street after their mother died. Another, who was turned out by her stepmother "because she had five of her own and could not afford to keep her," could not remember ever having been in church or Sunday-school, and only knew the name of Jesus through hearing people swear by it. She had no idea what they meant. These were specimens of the overflow from the tenements of our home-heathen that are growing up in New York's streets to-day, while tender-hearted men and women are busying themselves with the socks and the hereafter of well-fed little Hottentots thousands of miles away.

HANDOUT 11.3
CHAPTER 20 EXCERPTS:
"THE WORKING GIRLS OF NEW YORK"

It is estimated that at least one hundred and fifty thousand women and girls earn their own living in New York; but there is reason to believe that this estimate falls far short of the truth when sufficient account is taken of the large number who are not wholly dependent upon their own labor, while contributing by it to the family's earnings. These alone constitute a large class of the women wage-earners, and it is characteristic of the situation that the very fact that some need not starve on their wages condemns the rest to that fate. The pay they are willing to accept all have to take. What the "everlasting law of supply and demand," that serves as such a convenient gag for public indignation, has to do with it, one learns from observation all along the road of inquiry into these real woman's wrongs. To take the case of the saleswomen for illustration: The investigation of the Working Women's Society disclosed the fact that wages averaging from $2 to $4.50 a week were reduced by excessive fines, the employers placing a value upon time lost that is not given to services rendered." A little girl, who received two dollars a week, made cash-sales amounting to $167 in a single day, while the receipts of a fifteen-dollar male clerk in the same department footed up only $195; yet for some trivial mistake the girl was fined sixty cents out of her two dollars. The practice prevailed in some stores of dividing the fines between the superintendent and the time-keeper at the end of the year. In one instance they amounted to $3,000, and "the superintendent was heard to charge the timekeeper with not being strict enough in his duties." One of the causes for fine in a certain large store was sitting down. The law requiring seats for saleswomen, generally ignored, was obeyed faithfully in this establishment. The seats were there, but the girls were fined when found using them.

Cash-girls receiving $1.75 a week for work that at certain seasons lengthened their day to sixteen hours were sometimes required to pay for their aprons. A common cause for discharge from stores in which, on account of the oppressive heat and lack of ventilation, "girls fainted day after day and came out looking like corpses," was too long service. No other fault was found with the discharged saleswomen than that they had been long enough in the employ of the firm to justly expect an increase of salary. The reason was even given with brutal frankness, in some instances.

These facts give a slight idea of the hardships and the poor pay of a business that notoriously absorbs child-labor. The girls are sent to the store before they have fairly entered their teens, because the money they can earn there is needed for the support of the family. If the boys will not work, if the street tempts them from home, among the girls at least there must be no drones. To keep their places they are told to lie about their age and to say that they are over foul teen. The precaution is usually superfluous. The Women's Investigating Committee found the majority of the children employed in the stores to be under age, but heard only in a single instance of the truant officers calling. In that case they came once a year and sent the youngest children home; but in a month's time they were all back in their places, and were not again disturbed. When it comes to the factories, where hard bodily labor is added to long hours, stifling rooms, and starvation wages, matters are even worse. The Legislature has passed laws to pre-

HANDOUT 11.3, CONTINUED

vent the employment of children, as it has forbidden saloon-keepers to sell them beer, and it has provided means of enforcing its mandate, so efficient, that the very number of factories in New York is guessed at as in the neighborhood of twelve thousand. Up till this summer, a single inspector was charged with the duty of keeping the run of them all, and of seeing to it that the law was respected by the owners.

Sixty cents is put as the average day's earnings of the 150,000, but into this computation enters the stylish "cashier's" two dollars a day, as well as the thirty cents of the poor little girl who pulls threads in an East Side factory, and, if anything, the average is probably too high. . . . Two young sewing-girls came in seeking domestic service, so that they might get enough to eat. They had been only half-fed for some time, and starvation had driven them to the one door at which the pride of the American-born girl will not permit her to knock, though poverty be the price of her independence.

The tenement and the competition of public institutions and farmers' wives and daughters, have done the tyrant shirt to death, but they have not bettered the lot of the needle-women. The sweater of the East Side has appropriated the flannel shirt. He turns them out today at forty-five cents a dozen, paying his Jewish workers from twenty to thirty-five cents. One of these testified before the State Board of Arbitration, during the shirtmakers' strike, that she worked eleven hours in the shop and four at home, and had never in the best of times made over six dollars a week. Another stated that she worked from 4 o'clock in the morning to 11 at night. These girls had to find their own thread and pay for their own machines out of their wages. The white shirt has gone to the public and private institutions that shelter large numbers of young girls, and to the country. There are not half as many shirtmakers in New York to-day as only a few years ago, and some of the largest firms have closed their city shops. The same is true of the manufacturers of underwear. One large Broadway firm has nearly all its work done by farmers' girls in Maine, who think themselves well off if they can earn two or three dollars a week to pay for a Sunday silk, or the wedding outfit, little dreaming of the part they are playing in starving their city sisters Literally, they sew "with double thread, a shroud as well as a shirt." Their pin-money sets the rate of wages for thousands of poor sewing-girls in New York. The average earnings of the worker on underwear to-day do not exceed the three dollars which her competitor among the Eastern hills is willing to accept as the price of her play. The shirtmaker's pay is better only because the very finest custom work is all there is left for her to do.

1914-1945

CHAPTER 12

THE ERA OF WORLD WARS

But there is one front and one battle where everyone in the United States—every man, woman, and child—is in action, and will be privileged to remain in action throughout this war. That front is right here at home, in our daily lives, in our daily tasks.—Speech by Franklin Delano Roosevelt, April 28, 1942

HISTORICAL BACKGROUND: WHAT DO I NEED TO KNOW?

Entry onto the world stage in the 1880s and 1890s—the era of imperialism—brought the United States into contact with European nations in a new way. Although the U.S. engaged in trade with many different nations and stayed free of the "entangling alliances" that President Washington had wisely cautioned against, Europe had become divided into distinct alliances. In June 1914, the assassination of Archduke Ferdinand of Austria sparked war between Serbia and Austria-Hungary. Soon most of the world was engaged in World War I, which killed unprecedented numbers of men.

The United States maintained trade with different nations, selling arms to the Germans and British alike. Domestically, the nation debated neutrality. In response to German U-boat attacks against American ships carrying wartime supplies to England and to a German telegram promising the return of the Southwest United States if Mexico would join the war, the U.S. joined the war in 1917.

The U.S. government had grave concerns about the loyalty of a nation of immigrants—Irish Americans in particular strongly supported the Germans against the British. Other Americans simply felt that it was not in the nation's interest to join the war. To create support, the government turned to propaganda films, posters, and other media. Although late to the fighting, United States men and materials helped bring an end to the war.

Peace in 1918 brought American troops home. In 1919, a worldwide influenza epidemic, spread by wartime travel, eventually killed between fifty and one hundred million people, while fears of communism fanned the Red Scare in the United States. The 1920s saw both Prohibition and an economic boom that greatly benefitted urban Americans but left farmers behind. As a result, many Americans migrated from their farms to the cities, causing the agricultural sector of the economy to decline after 1925.

Unrestrained growth began to falter in 1929 as the economy contracted. Easy credit led to high debt, and speculation in stocks caused massive losses. As banks closed, employers began to lay off workers, contributing to a downward economic spiral. By 1932, despite some attempts by President Hoover's administration to remedy the situation, the United States and the world had entered a Great Depression.

No sector of the economy escaped the crash, but farmers were hit especially hard as price declines led them to plant more, which glutted the market and led to further declines. Droughts in 1934, 1936, and 1939 ruined crops in the Midwest. When poor soil conditions turned the soil to dust, fierce windstorms blew the top layer off of more than 100,000 acres in Oklahoma and the Midwest, creating what Americans called the Dustbowl.

In Europe in the meantime, old animosities, under pressure from the Great Depression and totalitarian Nazism in Germany, brought remilitarization and renewed war. In Asia the Japanese Empire expanded into European and American possessions, and Japan invaded China in 1937. By 1939 German tanks began to roll across Europe. As they had before World War I, most Americans preferred to stay out of the conflict, but sold weapons to England. However, a Japanese attack on Pearl Harbor on December 7, 1941, and a German declaration of war against the United States that same month brought the United States fully into the global conflict.

As American men and women marched off to war, those who remained on the home front became involved in the war effort. Women took work in the factories, while movies, posters, and advertisements exhorted men and women to work harder, remember the troops overseas, be aware of possible spies in their midst, and dedicate every facet of their lives to winning the war. No sector of the economy, no person who remained on the home front, and no part of society could escape that the United States was involved in total war.

After 1942 a steady string of Allied victories slowly pushed the Japanese and Germans back. Germany surrendered in May, 1945, and Japan followed suit in September. Having once again escaped the ravages of the battlefield, the United States emerged an economic and military powerhouse—a world power that late 19th-century imperialists could scarcely have foreseen.

STANDARDS ADDRESSED

NCHS—U.S. History Content Standards, Grades 5–12:
- How the United States changed from the end of World War I to the eve of the Great Depression
- The causes of the Great Depression and how it affected American society
- The causes and course of World War II, the character of the war at home and abroad, and its reshaping of the U.S. role in world affairs

CCSS for Literacy in History/Social Studies, Grades 6–8:
- Cite specific textual evidence to support analysis of primary and secondary sources.
- Determine the central ideas or information of a primary or secondary source; provide an accurate summary of the sources distinct from prior knowledge of opinions.
- Integrate visual information (e.g., in charts, graphs, photographs, videos, or maps) with the other information in print and digital texts.

LESSON 1

ORGANIZING QUESTION
How were propaganda techniques used in World War I to try to influence the public?

STRATEGIES USED
Quick Write, Think Aloud, Poster Analysis

MATERIALS NEEDED
1. One copy per student of these handouts:
   - ✓ "Propaganda Techniques" from the Public Broadcasting Service (n.d.a), available at http://www-tc.pbs.org/weta/reportingamerica atwar/teachers/pdf/propaganda.pdf
   - ✓ National Archives Poster Analysis Sheet, available at http://www. archives.gov/education/lessons/worksheets/poster_analysis_ worksheet.pdf

2. Color copies of the following propaganda posters sources or a classroom set of laptops or iPads for students to view them online:
   - ✓ Charles Bull's (1917) *Keep Him Free*, available at http://www.loc. gov/pictures/resource/cph.3b52634/
   - ✓ Henry Raleigh's (ca. 1918) *Halt the Hun*, available at http://www. loc.gov/pictures/resource/cph.3b48556/
   - ✓ Charles Chambers's (1917) *Food will win the war*, available at http:// www.loc.gov/pictures/resource/ppmsca.05651/
   - ✓ Harry Mueller's (1919) *Adventure and Action: Enlist in the Field Artillery, U.S. Army*, available at http://www.loc.gov/pictures/ resource/cph.3g07577/
   - ✓ P. G. Morgan's (1918) *Keep this Hand of Mercy at its Work*, available at http://www.loc.gov/pictures/resource/cph.3g07762/
   - ✓ Walter Whitehead's (1918) *Stand by the Boys in the Trenches—Mine More Coal*, available at http://www.loc.gov/pictures/resource/ cph.3g07924/
   - ✓ *Help to Catch Huns. Victory Bonds Shorten the War* (1918), available at http://www.loc.gov/pictures/resource/cph.3g12180/

✓ Fernand Gottlob's (1919) *Remember!*, available at http://www.loc.gov/pictures/resource/cph.3f03992/
✓ Theophile Steinlen's (1916) *Save Serbia Our Ally*, available at http://www.loc.gov/pictures/resource/cph.3f03989/
✓ Cushman Parker's (1917) *Little Americans Do Your Bit*, available at http://www.loc.gov/pictures/resource/cph.3g10218/
✓ Haskell Coffin's (1918) *Joan of Arc Saved France*, available at http://www.loc.gov/pictures/resource/cph.3b48466/

LESSON PLAN

Lesson Hook: *Quick Write*—Have students spend 5 minutes writing their responses to the following questions:
- What is your favorite commercial?
- What product is it advertising?
- What techniques are used to get you to buy the product?

Have students share their responses. Discuss with the class techniques that are used to make commercials memorable and to persuade the viewer to buy the product. Ask students for examples of other ways these techniques might be used, such as in political ads and speeches.

The Organizing Question: Explain that students will examine a variety of propaganda posters from the World War I era to determine the answer to the organizing question: How were propaganda techniques used in World War I to try to influence the public?

Examine the Sources: Give students copies of the List of Propaganda Techniques and the National Archives Poster Analysis sheet. Write the word "propaganda" on the board. Have students brainstorm definitions and examples. Discuss the list of propaganda techniques and ask students to generate some modern examples of each one. Explain that they are going to work in groups to analyze a poster for symbols and propaganda techniques used, the target audience, and the message or purpose of the poster.

Think Aloud—Display Charles Bull's (1917) *Keep Him Free* on a screen. Using the Poster Analysis sheet, do a think aloud with students and model how to analyze a poster using the template. Allow students to help with some of the questions as the class works through the sample together.

Poster Analysis—Next, divide the class into 10 groups and give each group a color copy of one of the propaganda posters or a technology device to view an electronic version of the poster. Their task is to work in their group to complete the Poster Analysis sheet for their propaganda poster. When the sheet is completed, have groups use the list of propaganda techniques to determine what techniques were used in their poster.

Make a Hypothesis: Once all of the groups have finished, allow each group to share its poster and responses to the questions. Remind students of the organizing question for the lesson and the list of propaganda techniques. Encourage them to write down clues from the group presentations that might help answer the question. Display online versions of the images on a screen, so all of the class can see the details as the groups present. After presentations, have each group work together to create a hypothesis that answers the organizing question; require three or four examples of images as evidence. An optional extension of this lesson would be to have students design their own propaganda poster using one or two of the propaganda techniques.

LESSON 2

ORGANIZING QUESTION

How did popular culture in the 1930s reflect the effects of the Great Depression?

STRATEGIES USED

Brainstorming, Primary Source Analysis, Collaborative Groups

MATERIALS NEEDED

1. Two or three copies per group of each of the following Library of Congress Primary Source Analysis Template:
   - ✓ Analyzing Photographs and Prints, available at http://www.loc.gov/teachers/usingprimarysources/resources/Analyzing_Photographs_and_Prints.pdf
   - ✓ Analyzing Primary Sources (for Groups 3 and 4), available at http://www.loc.gov/teachers/usingprimarysources/resources/Analyzing_Primary_Sources.pdf
   - ✓ Analyzing Sheet Music and Song Sheets, available at http://www.loc.gov/teachers/usingprimarysources/resources/Analyzing_Sheet_Music_and_Song_Sheets.pdf
   - ✓ Analyzing Political Cartoons, available at http://www.loc.gov/teachers/usingprimarysources/resources/Analyzing_Political_Cartoons.pdf

2. Two color copies of each of these sources, organized into sets by type of source, and placed in eight envelopes:
   - ✓ Photographs Set (For Groups 1 and 2):
     - » Dorothea Lange's *Example of Self-Resettlement in California* (1936b), available at http://www.loc.gov/pictures/resource/fsa.8b38486/
     - » Dorothea Lange's (1936a) *Destitute Pea Pickers in California. Mother of Seven Children*, available at http://www.loc.gov/pictures/resource/fsa.8b29516/
     - » Dorothea Lange's (1936c) *Migrant Agricultural Worker's Family*, available at http://www.loc.gov/pictures/resource/ppmsca.03054/

» Dorothea Lange's (1935) *Oklahoma Dust Bowl Refugees. San Fernando, California*, available at http://www.loc.gov/pictures/resource/fsa.8b27316/

» Carl Mydans's (1935) *CCC (Civilian Conservation Corps) Workers, Prince George's County, Maryland*, available at http://www.loc.gov/pictures/resource/fsa.8a00073/

✓ Poster Set (For Groups 3 and 4):

» Albert Bender's (1941) *A Young Man's Opportunity for Work, Play, Study & Health*, available at http://lcweb2.loc.gov/service/pnp/ppmsca/12800/12896v.jpg

» Albert Bender's (ca. 1939) *Jobs for Girls & Women*, available at http://www.loc.gov/pictures/resource/cph.3b53089/

» Federal Art Project's (ca. 1936) *Keep Your Fire Escapes Clear*, available at http://www.loc.gov/pictures/resource/ds.05007/

» Fred Rentschler's (1938) *This is an Adult World, Its Problems Are Up to You!*, available at http://www.loc.gov/pictures/resource/cph.3f05422/

» Benjamin Sheer's (1936) *Better Housing: The Solution to Infant Mortality in the Slums*, available at http://www.loc.gov/pictures/resource/cph.3f05647/

✓ Music Set (For Groups 5 and 6):

» Lester Hunter's (1938) "I'd Rather Not Be On Relief," available at http://www.loc.gov/teachers/classroommaterials/primarysourcesets/dust-bowl-migration/pdf/relief.pdf

» Flora Robertson's (ca. 1940) "Why we Come to Californy," available at http://www.loc.gov/teachers/classroommaterials/primarysourcesets/dust-bowl-migration/pdf/californy.pdf

» Mary Sullivan's (ca. 1930s) "Sunny California," available at http://www.loc.gov/teachers/lyrical/songs/docs/california_trans.pdf

✓ Political Cartoon Set (For Groups 7 and 8):

» Herbert Block's (1930) "The philanthropist," available at http://www.loc.gov/pictures/item/00652174/

» John McCutcheon's (ca. 1931) "A Wise Economist Asks a Question," available at http://www.loc.gov/pictures/item/acd1996005778/PP/

» Clifford Kennedy Berryman's (1930) "Awful job to quiet anything around here!," available at http://www.loc.gov/pictures/item/acd1996001381/pp/

LESSON PLAN

Lesson Hook: *Brainstorming*—Ask students to pretend that an alien from the future has landed on Earth and wants to understand the culture of children their age in the United States. Have them brainstorm in their notes all of the things the alien needs to know to be able to fit in. After students make a list, have them share their responses and write them on the board. Prompt them to think about music, movies, books, food, leisure activities, technology, and clothing. Clarify that these are all elements of "popular culture" that vary through different times and places in history.

The Organizing Question: Explain that students will examine pictures, posters, song lyrics, and political cartoons for clues to answer the organizing question: How did popular culture in the 1930s reflect the effects of the Great Depression?

Examine the Sources: *Primary Source Analysis/Collaborative Groups*—Divide the class into eight groups and give each group an envelope of sources (images, posters, music, and political cartoons). Also give students in each group a copy of the Primary Source Analysis Guide that matches their source set. Explain that they are to examine the sources in the envelope using the Analysis Template. They do not have to answer all of the questions, but they should use the question prompts in the Observe, Reflect, and Question sections to help them figure out their images. Have the students make a list of patterns they see in their group of sources. While they are working, remind them of the organizing question for the lesson.

Make a Hypothesis: Once students are finished discussing each of their images, have them create a hypothesis as a group that answers the organizing question. They should list specific examples from their sources to support the hypothesis. Bring the class back together into a whole group circle and have each group share its hypothesis and sources. Show online versions or use a document camera so all group members can see each image. Ask students to listen for similarities from all of the sources. Make a list on the board of these similarities and what they reveal about popular culture in the 1930s. Compare and contrast the 1930s list to their brainstormed list about modern popular culture from the lesson hook activity.

LESSON 3

ORGANIZING QUESTION

How did different people experience the home front during World War II?

STRATEGIES USED

Gallery Walk, Analyzing Oral Histories

MATERIALS NEEDED

1. One copy of each of these images posted around the room in stations:
    ✓ Poster: U.S. Office of War Information's (1943) *Do with Less*, available at http://www.loc.gov/pictures/resource/fsa.8b06175/
    ✓ Poster: *Are you doing all you can?* (1942), available at http://loc.gov/pictures/item/99400737/
    ✓ Poster: William Tasker's (ca. 1942) *Service on the Homefront*, available at http://www.loc.gov/pictures/resource/cph.3b49007/
    ✓ Poster: Federal Art Project's (ca. 1942) *Save Scrap for Victory*, available at http://www.loc.gov/pictures/resource/cph.3f05676/
    ✓ Poster: *War Gardens for Victory* (ca. 1942), available at http://www.loc.gov/pictures/resource/cph.3g04436/
    ✓ Poster: Bressler Editorial Cartoons's (ca. 1944) *Good work, sister! we never figured you could do a man-size job!*, available at http://loc.gov/pictures/resource/cph.3g05597/
    ✓ Photograph: Ansel Adams's (1943) *Entrance to Manzanar: Manzanar Relocation Center*, available at http://www.loc.gov/pictures/resource/ppprs.00286/?co=manz

2. Chart paper and markers (Place a piece of chart paper beside each image posted in the Gallery Walk stations.)
3. One copy for each student of the Library of Congress Analyzing Oral Histories Template, available at http://www.loc.gov/teachers/usingprimarysources/resources/Analyzing_Oral_Histories.pdf
4. Either printed copies of each source or laptops/iPads to view these sources online:
    ✓ Interview: Archie Miyatake (n.d.), http://www.janm.org/exhibits/breed/interv.htm (*Note*: Have students read the Biographical

Information, Departure for Camp, Life in Camp, and Returning Home sections.)

✓ Oral histories: "What did you do in the war, Grandma? Oral Histories of Rhode Island Women in WWII" (1995), available at http://cds.library.brown.edu/projects/WWII_Women/tocCS.html (*Note*: This site contains transcripts of interviews with 26 women in World War II. Either assign an interview for students to examine or allow them to choose based on the title of the interview.)

✓ Interviews from PBS's (n.d.b) The War Project, available at http://www.pbs.org/thewar/the_witnesses_homefront.htm (*Note*: This site contains interviews and artifacts from 15 people from World War II. Either assign one for students to examine or allow them to choose.)

LESSON PLAN

Lesson Hook: Begin class by showing either a personal family picture from the past or historical photos of your community 50 or 100 years ago. Tell a story that you remember from an older relative or share a childhood memory. Ask students if they have parents, grandparents, or elderly friends who have shared stories about their past or memories of growing up. Allow students to share these stories. Once several students have responded, share that these stories are oral histories of a particular time and place.

The Organizing Question: Explain that students will examine images and oral histories of people who lived during the war era to answer the organizing question: How did different people experience the home front during World War II?

Examine the Sources: *Gallery Walk*—Begin this part of the lesson by reviewing what "home front" means when talking about a war. Tell students that they will participate in a Gallery Walk and examine images to predict some ways that people on the home front were affected by events in World War II. Have students choose a partner, give each pair a marker, and then assign the pairs to a station to start the Gallery Walk. Their task is to examine the image first, then write on the chart paper what they notice and what they think it tells them about effects of the war on events at home. Have the students rotate clockwise, adding their comments and responding to others' written ideas. When they have returned to the image where they started, have them read all of the responses and report to the class what they think the image tells them about life on the home front.

Analyzing Oral Histories—Have students stay with their partners for this section of the lesson. Begin by asking students why oral histories might be beneficial to help understand a certain time period or event. Explain that now they will look at either written transcripts or audio recordings of oral history interviews from people who lived during the war. Give each student a copy of the Analyzing Oral Histories Template. Choose one of the interview transcripts from the "What did you do in the war, Grandma?" site and model how to analyze an oral history using the Observe, Reflect, and Question sample questions on the template. Make adjustments to the questions as needed based on whether the interview is in written or audio format. Either assign sources or allow students to choose which interview they would like to listen to or read. Once that is done, provide paper copies or electronic devices for online viewing of the oral histories and interviews listed at the end of the Materials Needed Section.

Have students work with their partner to either read or listen to the oral history, using questions from the Analyzing Oral History Template to guide their analysis. If students finish early, have them examine another source. Once all pairs are finished, have them share information about their source/person with the whole class.

Make a Hypothesis: Once all students have shared their sources, write the organizing question on the board. Allow students to make a hypothesis with their partner, using evidence from the oral histories. After a few minutes of thinking in small groups, have a whole-class discussion and write their hypotheses with evidence on the board while students write examples in their notes. Discuss their responses and have students make connections to the images they examined in the Gallery Walk. Ask them to assess whether or not their conclusions about the visual images were supported by the oral histories they examined.

1940-1970

CHAPTER 13

CIVIL RIGHTS

"I say to you today, my friends, so even though we face the difficulties of today and tomorrow, I still have a dream. It is a dream deeply rooted in the American dream. I have a dream that one day this nation will rise up and live out the true meaning of its creed: 'We hold these truths to be self-evident: that all men are created equal."—Martin Luther King, Jr., "I Have A Dream" Speech, August 28, 1963

HISTORICAL BACKGROUND: WHAT DO I NEED TO KNOW?

Months before the United States entered World War II, President Franklin Roosevelt gave his 1941 State of the Union Address. The Four Freedoms Speech outlined what Roosevelt viewed as fundamental human rights: freedom of speech, freedom of worship, freedom from want, freedom from fear. During the war, the United States made calls for liberty, equality, and freedom for all peoples a central part of its philosophical campaign.

But although U.S. and Allied troops fought against the Germans and Japanese, non-White Americans on the home front experienced racial inequality. Beginning in the 1870s, Jim Crow laws relegated African Americans to so-called "separate but equal" status. State laws in the South required, among other things, separate entrances in movie theaters, separate drinking fountains, separate seating in diners and restaurants, separate cars on trains, and separate public busses.

Starting in the 1950s, African Americans and Whites began to organize effective civil rights campaigns across the South. A key component of the campaign was the philosophy of civil disobedience and nonviolence successfully employed by Mahatma Ghandi in India. Protestors were instructed to dress well, be neat in appearance, polite, and above all to never engage in any kind of violence.

A series of events seemed to indicate a quickening pace for the Civil Rights Movement. In 1955, Rosa Parks refused to surrender her seat on a Montgomery, AL, bus, sparking her arrest and a successful boycott of the public bus system by African Americans. When Arkansas Governor Orville Faubus tried to use National Guard troops to prevent integration of Little Rock schools, President Eisenhower nationalized the Guard and activated the U.S. Army to ensure compliance. A series of lunch counter sit-ins by African Americans across the South successfully desegregated eating many establishments.

In the early 1960s national civil rights groups as well as Black and White students from across the U.S. worked to register African Americans disenfranchised by restrictive voting rights laws. They were frequently met with sometimes extreme violence. In 1963, civil rights leader Martin Luther King, Jr., gave his "I Have a Dream" speech on the steps of the Lincoln Memorial, outlining his vision for equality in America. After his arrest later that year in Birmingham, AL, a horrified national television audience watched as local police used fire hoses and dogs to attack children, teenagers, and adults peacefully demonstrating for their Constitutional rights. Meanwhile, the Soviet Union employed Cold War propaganda to argue that Soviet citizens enjoyed more equality than those in supposedly democratic America. Worried about its status as "leader of the free world," American politicians began to argue for a series of national civil rights laws.

Following President John F. Kennedy's assassination in 1963, President Lyndon B. Johnson, from Texas, pushed for civil rights legislation to right the wrongs of racial discrimination and to honor Kennedy's memory. The Civil Rights Act of 1964, first proposed by Kennedy in 1963, outlawed discrimination based on race, sex, nationality, or religion. The Voting Rights Act of 1965 allowed the government to enforce Constitutional voting rights and regulate elections in states found out of compliance, while the Civil Rights Act of 1968 required fair housing practices.

For some, the Civil Rights Era had achieved major gains. For others, the progress was neither far nor fast enough. Many African Americans had migrated to northern and western cities during the Depression and World War

II, and they found a system of discrimination as well as high unemployment, and police forces that did not match the racial make-up of the cities. Racial tension exploded in a series of race riots between 1964 and 1968. Likewise, some African American leaders, such as Malcom X and leaders of Black Power groups like the Black Panthers, did not believe in King's nonviolent philosophies. For them equality needed to be seized, not requested. By the early 1970s, the Civil Rights Movement had fragmented, with each faction employing different philosophies working toward the same ultimate goal—equality for all.

STANDARDS ADDRESSED

NCHS U.S. History Content Standards, Grades 5–12:

- The struggle for racial and gender equality and the extension of civil liberties

CCSS for Literacy in History/Social Studies, Grades 6–8:

- Integrate visual information (e.g., in charts, graphs, photographs, videos, or maps) with other information in print and digital texts.
- Determine the central ideas or information of a primary or secondary source: provide an accurate summary of the source distinct from prior knowledge or opinions.
- Identify aspects of a text that reveal an author's point of view or purpose (e.g., loaded language, inclusion or avoidance of particular facts).

LESSON 1

ORGANIZING QUESTION

What changes were needed for African Americans in the U.S. in the 1950s and 1960s?

STRATEGIES USED

Brainstorming, Think Aloud, Gallery Walk

MATERIALS NEEDED

1. One copy per student of the Three-Column Notes Guide (**Handout 13.1**)
2. Laws: Three or four examples of Jim Crow laws (National Park Service, n.d.b) per group, printed and cut into strips, available at http://www.nps. gov/malu/forteachers/jim_crow_laws.htm
3. One copy of each of the following images posted on the wall or in stations around the room (*Note*: All photographs are from the Enforcing Racial Discrimination Collection at the Library of Congress):
    ✓ Jack Delano's (1940b) *At the Bus Station*, available at http://www. loc.gov/pictures/item/fsa1998006256/PP/
    ✓ Esther Bubley's (1943) *People Waiting for a Bus at the Greyhound Bus Terminal*, available at http://www.loc.gov/rr/print/list/085_ disc.html
    ✓ Jack Delano's (1940b) *A Café Near the Tobacco Market*, available at http://www.loc.gov/pictures/item/fsa1998006213/PP
    ✓ John Vachon's (1938b) *Drinking Fountain on the County Courthouse Lawn*, available at http://www.loc.gov/pictures/item/ fsa1997003218/PP/
    ✓ Marion Post Wolcott's (1939b) *Negro Going in Colored Entrance of Movie House on Saturday Afternoon, Balzoni, Mississippi Delta, Mississippi*, available at http://www.loc.gov/picrures/item/ fsa1998013484/PP/
    ✓ Marion Post Wolcott's (1939a) *Beale Street, Memphis, Tennessee*, available at http://www.loc.gov/pictures/item/fsa1998013763/PP/
    ✓ John Vachon's (1938a) *Railroad Station, Manchester, Georgia*, available at http://www.loc.gov/pictures/item/fsa1997003449/PP/
    ✓ *Ronald Martin, Robert Patterson, and Mark Martin Stage Sit-Down Strike After Being Refused Service at a F.W. Woolworth Luncheon*

Counter, Greensboro, N.C. (1960), available at http://www.loc.gov/exhibits/odyssey/archive/09/0909001r.jpg

LESSON PLAN

Lesson Hook: *Brainstorming*—Ask students what changes they would like to see in their school, city, state, or nation. Have them brainstorm some possible problems that might need changes at any of these levels, who would be responsible for bringing about these changes, and what strategies he or she might use. List their ideas on the board as they brainstorm.

The Organizing Question: Explain that students will examine several images and laws to answer the organizing question: What changes were needed for African Americans in the 1950s and 1960s?

Examine the Sources: Distribute a copy of **Handout 13.1** and explain how students will use it for all three lessons about civil rights.

Think Aloud—Display *At the Bus Station* (Delano, 1940b) on a screen. Do a Think Aloud with students to model what you notice in the image and what questions you have. Encourage students to add observations and record evidence and sources on the notes guide.

Gallery Walk—Explain to students that they will circulate around the room, spend one or two minutes looking at each image, and record evidence and sources on **Handout 13.1**. At the last station, groups should report their evidence to the class. Ask students how they might find out more information about what is happening in the images. Use their responses to introduce the next clues.

Provide students with background on Jim Crow laws. Tell them they will examine some laws to find more evidence to help answer the organizing question. Put students into groups and give each group three or four laws to examine. Student groups should summarize their laws, fill in details on the notes guide, and be ready to report the main ideas of the laws to the whole class.

Make a Hypothesis: Either in writing or as a whole-class discussion, have students use **Handout 13.1** to make a hypothesis about the organizing question. Prompt students to discuss connections between the images and the Jim Crow laws and to cite evidence from the sources to support their responses.

HANDOUT 13.1
THREE-COLUMN NOTES GUIDE

How much progress has the U.S. made toward Martin Luther King, Jr.'s dream?

What changes needed to be made for African Americans in the U.S.? (Source?)	What was Martin Luther King, Jr.'s vision for change? (Source?)	What strategies were used to bring about change during the Civil Rights Movement? (Source?)

LESSON 2

ORGANIZING QUESTION
What was Martin Luther King, Jr.'s vision for change in the U.S.?

STRATEGIES USED
Free Writing, Reciprocal Reading

MATERIALS NEEDED
1. One copy of Martin Luther King, Jr.'s (1963) "I Have a Dream" speech, available at http://www.archives.gov/press/exhibits/dream-speech.pdf (*Note*: Divide the speech into five sections or chunks, depending on the reading levels of your students, and number them from 1 to 5.)
2. Video of the speech, available on several online sites
3. Construction paper
4. **Handout 13.1**

LESSON PLAN

Lesson Hook: *Free Writing*—Begin class by having students write a response to this prompt for 5 minutes:

> I have a dream that one day . . .

Discuss their responses and ask where students have previously heard this phrase. Have the class brainstorm a list of things they remember about Martin Luther King, Jr.

The Organizing Question: Explain that they will examine the speech to answer the organizing question for this lesson: What was Martin Luther King, Jr.'s vision for change in the U.S.?

Examine the Sources: Explain background information and the context of King's (1963) "I Have a Dream" speech. Show a few minutes of the video of King's speech. Have students give their reaction to what they heard or noticed about the content, the way the speech was delivered, the crowd, and King himself. Explain to students that they will now look at a written version of the speech for clues to answer the question. Read the first section or chunk of the speech aloud and model summarizing for the students.

Reciprocal Reading—Divide the class into groups of four and have students use the following reciprocal reading strategies to discuss the speech:

- The first group member reads a paragraph or chunk.
- The second group member summarizes what was just read.
- The third group member makes connections between what was read and what was learned from the images or Jim Crow laws in Lesson 1.
- The fourth group member makes a prediction about what might come next or poses a question. Then the members rotate roles and go on to the next section or chunk.

Give groups time to read and discuss the speech using these roles. Once they have finished their reading and discussion, students should add the evidence in column two of **Handout 13.1**. While they are working, circulate to clarify any misconceptions or answer questions.

Make a Hypothesis: Have each reciprocal reading group create a visual on construction paper that depicts Martin Luther King, Jr.'s vision or dream for change. They must be able to explain their visual with evidence from the speech. Ask students to compare and contrast his "I have a dream" phrases with their writing from the lesson hook.

LESSON 3

ORGANIZING QUESTION

What strategies were used to bring about change for African Americans?

STRATEGIES USED

List-Group-Label, Picture Prediction, Annotating a Text

MATERIALS NEEDED

1. **Handout 13.1**
2. Locate the following images online to display on a screen:
   - ✓ Photograph: *Ronald Martin, Robert Patterson, and Mark Martin Stage Sit-Down Strike After Being Refused Service at a F.W. Woolworth Luncheon Counter, Greensboro, N.C.* (1960), available at http://www.loc.gov/exhibits/odyssey/archive/09/0909001r.jpg
   - ✓ Photograph: Warren Leffler's (1963) *Civil Rights March on Washington, D.C.,* available at http://www.loc.gov/pictures/resource/ppmsca.03128/
   - ✓ Photograph: *Black Panther Party* (n.d.), available at http://en.wikipedia.org/wiki/File:Black-Panther-Party-armed-guards-in-street-shotguns.jpg
   - ✓ Public Report: Arrest of Rosa Parks (1955), available at http://www.archives.gov/global-pages/larger-image.html?i=/education/lessons/rosa-parks/images/police-report-l.jpg&c=/education/lessons/rosa-parks/images/police-report.caption.html
   - ✓ Photograph: *Woman fingerprinted. Mrs. Rosa Parks, Negro seamstress, whose refusal to move to the back of a bus touched off the bus boycott in Montgomery, Ala.* (1956), available at http://www.loc.gov/pictures/item/94500293/?sid=61c69742c46cd2d89737b98496366177
   - ✓ Newspaper article: President Truman Wipes Out Segregation in Armed Forces (1948), available at http://www.loc.gov/exhibits/odyssey/archive/09/0902001r.jpg
   - ✓ Newspaper article: 5,000 at Meeting Outline Boycott; Bullet Clips Bus (1955), available at http://www.loc.gov/exhibits/odyssey/archive/09/0903001r.jpg

✓ Newspaper article: Segregation in Schools is Outlawed (1954), available at http://www.loc.gov/exhibits/brown/brown-brown.html

✓ Photograph: O. J. Rapp's (1964) *President Johnson Signs the Civil Rights Act of 1964*, available at http://www.lbjlibrary.net/collections/photo-archive.html

- Copies for each group of one section of the Civil Rights Act of 1964, available at http://www.senate.gov/artandhistory/history/resources/pdf/CivilRightsActOf1964.pdf (*Note*: Divide the Act into five sections, Titles I–V. Give each group member a copy of his or her assigned section.)

LESSON PLAN

Lesson Hook: *List-Group-Label*—At this point in the year, students have studied many historical eras, people, and events. Explain to them that they will have 2 minutes to work with a partner and to write down as many examples as they can of "change" that has happened in history. After 2 minutes, have students identify patterns or similarities and group their examples into categories. If needed, prompt them to think about strategies used to bring about these changes, such as laws, wars, and protests. Next, have them create a label for each of their categories. Allow students freedom to create their own patterns and categories as long as they can explain their thinking to the class.

The Organizing Question: Explain that students will examine images and laws to answer the organizing question: What strategies were used to bring about change for African Americans?

Examine the Sources: Begin this part of the lesson by reviewing changes that were needed for African Americans from Lessons 1 and 2.

Picture Prediction—Show the images listed in the Materials Needed section on a screen. As you display each image, ask students these questions:
- What do you think is happening in this image?
- What evidence in the image leads you to think that?
- What strategy to bring about change might be occurring in this image?

As students respond to these images, have them write down the strategies for change on **Handout 13.1**. Explain some of the strategies and how they were important in the Civil Rights Movement (e.g., protests, boycotts, marches, sit-ins, legislation, etc.) Show *President Johnson Signs the Civil Rights Act of 1964* (Rapp, 1964) last as an introduction to the law.

Annotating a Text—Divide the class into five groups and give each group one of the sections of the Civil Rights Act (Titles I–V). Explain that the Civil Rights Act of 1964 was a major milestone in the Civil Rights Movement. Challenge students to examine their section of the Act for clues as to what changes were made for African Americans. While they are reading, have them complete these annotations for their section:

- Underline the major provisions, or changes made, in the law.
- In the margins of the text, write any questions they have and connections to previous sources used, such as images, Jim Crow laws, and the "I Have a Dream" speech.

Circulate and help with vocabulary words and difficult passages. Have each group report its findings about changes made in the law while the rest of the class writes these changes on **Handout 13.1**.

Make a Hypothesis: As either a class discussion or a writing task, have students use **Handout 13.1** to summarize strategies used to bring about change during the Civil Rights Movement. Lead the students in a discussion about what changes might still be needed in the U.S. Review Martin Luther King, Jr.'s vision for change. Have students discuss whether or not his vision has been achieved in the U.S. and what an "I Have a Dream" speech might include if it were written today.

REFERENCES

5,000 at meeting outline boycott; Bullet clips bus. (1955, Dec. 6). *The Montgomery Advertiser*. Library of Congress, Washington, D.C. Retrieved from http://www.loc.gov/exhibits/odyssey/archive/09/0903001r.jpg

The able doctor, or, America swallowing the bitter draught. (1774, May 1). Library of Congress, Washington, D.C. Retrieved from http://www.loc.gov/resource/cph.3g05289/

Adams, A. (1943). *Entrance to Manzanar: Manzanar Relocation Center*. Library of Congress, Washington, D.C. Retrieved from http://www.loc.gov/pictures/resource/ppprs.00286/?co=manz

Adams, J. (1818, Feb. 13). Correspondence. Retrieved from http://teaching americanhistory.org/library/document/john-adams-to-h-niles/

Alfred Murphy, an ex-slave. (n.d.). Ohio Historical Society Archives Library. Columbus, OH. Retrieved from http://dbs.ohiohistory.org/africanam/html/page857b.html?ID=4426

An Ordinance and Constitution for Council and Assembly in Virginia. (1621, July 24). Retrieved from http://www.gutenberg.org/files/36181/36181h/36181-h.htm#pg_10

Archer, G. (1998). A brief description of the people. In E. W. Haile (Ed.), *Jamestown narratives: Eyewitness accounts of the Virginia Colony, the first decade: 1607–1617* (pp. 122–124). Champlain, VA: Round House. [Original work published in 1607]

Are you doing all you can? (1942). Library of Congress, Washington, D.C. Retrieved from http://loc.gov/pictures/item/99400737/

Arrest of Rosa Parks. (1955, Dec. 1). National Archives, Washington, D.C. Retrieved from http://www.archives.gov/global-pages/larger-image.html?i=/education/lessons/rosa-parks/images/police-report-l.jpg&c=/education/lessons/rosa-parks/images/police-report.caption.html

Bartholomew, C. (1898, May 7). Will wear the stars and stripes. United States House of Representatives Office of Art & Archives. Retrieved from http://history.house.gov/Exhibitions-and-Publications/HAIC/Historical-Essays/Foreign-Domestic/Legislative-Interests/

Bender, A. (ca. 1939). *Jobs for girls & women*. Library of Congress, Washington, D.C. Retrieved from http://www.loc.gov/pictures/resource/cph.3b53089/

Bender, A. (1941). *A young man's opportunity for work, play, study & health*. Library of Congress, Washington, D.C. Retrieved from http://lcweb2.loc.gov/service/pnp/ppmsca/12800/12896v.jpg

Berryman, C. K. (1930). Awful job to quiet anything around here! Library of Congress, Washington, D.C. Retrieved from http://www.loc.gov/pictures/item/acd1996001381/pp/

Bierstadt, B. (1859, Aug. 13). *Crossing the Platte*. Retrieved from http://thewest.harpweek.com/Illustrations/!ListOfIllusHeader.htm

Bierstadt, A. (1863). *The Rocky Mountains, Lander's Peak* [Painting]. The Metropolitan Museum of Art, New York, NY. Retrieved from http://www.metmuseum.org/toah/works-of-art/07.123

Bierstadt, A. (1868). *Among the Sierra Nevada, California* [Painting]. Smithsonian American Art Museum, Washington, D.C. Retrieved from http://americanart.si.edu/t2go/1lw/index-noframe.html?/t2go/1lw/lw-index.html

Bixby, L., (1852, May 22). Correspondence. Center for Lowell History Collection, University of Massachusetts, Lowell, MA. Retrieved from http://libweb.uml.edu/clh/All/bix1.htm

Black Panther Party. (n.d.) Retrieved from http://en.wikipedia.org/wiki/File:Black-Panther-Party-armed-guards-in-street-shotguns.jpg

Block, H. (1930). The philanthropist. Library of Congress, Washington, D.C. Retrieved from http://www.loc.gov/pictures/item/00652174/

Boott Mills 1890s employees. (n.d.). University of Massachusetts, Lowell, MA. Retrieved from http://libweb.uml.edu/clh/All/mi07.htm

Bradford, W. (1908). Of Plymouth Plantation. Book 2. In W. T. Davis (Ed.), *Bradford's History of Plymouth Plantation, 1606–1646*. New York, NY: Charles Scribner's Sons. Retrieved from http://mith.umd.edu/eada/html/display.php?docs=bradford_history.xml [Original work published in 1630–1647]

Bressler Editorial Cartoons. (ca. 1944). *Good work, sister! we never figured you could do a man-size job!* Library of Congress, Washington, D.C. Retrieved from http://loc.gov/pictures/resource/cph.3g05597/

Bubley, E. (1943). *People waiting for a bus at the Greyhound bus terminal.* Retrieved from http://www.loc.gov/rr/print/list/085_disc.html

Bull, C. (1917) *Keep him free.* Library of Congress, Washington, D.C. Retrieved from http://www.loc.gov/pictures/resource/cph.3b52634/

Centennial mirror. (n.d.). Library of Congress, Washington, D.C. Retrieved from http://www.loc.gov/pictures/resource/cph.3b52134/

Chambers, C. (1917). *Food will win the war.* Library of Congress, Washington, D.C. Retrieved from http://www.loc.gov/pictures/resource/ppmsca.05651/

Civil Rights Act of 1964. (1964). Retrieved from http://www.senate.gov/artandhistory/history/resources/pdf/CivilRightsActOf1964.pdf

Coffin, H. (1918). *Joan of Arc saved France.* Library of Congress, Washington, D.C. Retrieved from http://www.loc.gov/pictures/resource/cph.3b48466/

Cole, N. (1967). Spiritual travels. In A. Heimert and P. Miller (Eds.), *The Great Awakening: Documents illustrating the crisis and its consequences* (pp. 183–186). New York, NY: The Bobbs-Merrill Company. [Original document published ca. 1740]

Cole, T. (1836). *View from Mount Holyoke, Northampton, Massachusetts, after a thunderstorm—the oxbow* [Painting]. The Metropolitan Museum of Art, New York, NY. Retrieved from http://www.metmuseum.org/toah/works-of-art/08.228

Cole, T. (1846). *The mountain ford* [Painting]. The Metropolitan Museum of Art, New York, NY. Retrieved from http://www.metmuseum.org/toah/works-of-art/15.30.63

Columbus, C. (1820). *Personal narrative of the first voyage of Columbus to America.* Boston, MA: Thomas B. Wait and Son. Retrieved from https://archive.org/details/personalnarrativ00colu

Confederate States of America. (n.d.). *A declaration of the immediate causes which induce and justify the secession of the state of Mississippi from the Federal Union.* Yale Law School, Lillian Goldman Law Library, New Haven, CT. Retrieved from http://avalon.law.yale.edu/19th_century/csa_missec.asp

Confederate States of America. (1860). *Declaration of the immediate causes which induce and justify the secession of South Carolina from the Federal Union.* Yale Law School, Lillian Goldman Law Library, New Haven, CT. Retrieved from http://avalon.law.yale.edu/19th_century/csa_scarsec.asp

Confederate States of America. (1861a). *A declaration of the causes which impel the state of Texas to secede from the Federal Union.* Yale Law School, Lillian

Goldman Law Library, New Haven, CT. Retrieved from http://avalon.law. yale.edu/19th_century/csa_texsec.asp

Confederate States of America. (1861b). Georgia secession. Yale Law School, Lillian Goldman Law Library, New Haven, CT. Retrieved from http://avalon.law.yale.edu/19th_century/csa_geosec.asp

Currier & Ives. (ca. 1876). *The stride of a century.* Library of Congress, Washington, D.C. Retrieved from http://www.loc.gov/pictures/item/93506699/

Dalrymple, L. (1899, Jan. 25). School begins. Library of Congress, Washington, D.C. Retrieved from http://www.loc.gov/pictures/resource/ppmsca.28668/

Dalrymple, L. (1905). The world's constable. Library of Congress, Washington, D.C. Retrieved from http://www.loc.gov/pictures/resource/ds.05213/

Davis, T. (1869, June 12). *Pilgrims on the plain.* Retrieved from http://thewest. harpweek.com/Illustrations/!ListOfIllusHeader.htm

de Bry, T. (ca. 1570–1590). Powhatan Indian Collection from watercolors by John White. Discovering Jamestown Gallery, Jamestown Settlement, VA. Retrieved from http://historyisfun.org/jamestown2007/imagegalleries/Powhatans/album/gallery.html

Declaration of Independence. (1776, July 4). National Archives, Washington, D.C. Retrieved from http://www.archives.gov/exhibits/charters/declaration_transcript.html

Delano, J. (1940a). *A café near the tobacco market.* Retrieved from http://www.loc.gov/pictures/item/fsa1998006213/PP/

Delano, J. (1940b). *At the bus station.* Retrieved from http://www.loc.gov/pictures/item/fsa1998006256/PP/

Destruction of the depots, public buildings, and manufactories at Atlanta, Georgia, November 15, 1864 and *The Fourteenth* and *Twentieth Corps moving out of Atlanta, November 15, 1864.* (1864). Library of Congress, Washington, D.C. Retrieved from http://www.loc.gov/pictures/item/00652832/

Drake, R. (1860). *Scene in the hold of the "Blood-Stained Gloria" (Middle Passage).* Virginia Foundation for the Humanities and University of Virginia Library, Charlottesville, VA. Retrieved from http://hitchcock.itc.virginia.edu/SlaveTrade/collection/large/E017.JPG

Durand, A. (1845). *The beeches* [Painting]. The Metropolitan Museum of Art, New York, NY. Retrieved from http://www.metmuseum.org/toah/works-of-art/15.30.59

Durand, A. (1849). *Kindred spirits* [Painting]. The Metropolitan Museum of Art, New York, NY. Retrieved from http://www.metmuseum.org/toah/works-of-art/L.2008.21

Durand, A. (1855). *In the woods* [Painting]. The Metropolitan Museum of Art, New York, NY. Retrieved from http://www.metmuseum.org/toah/works-of-art/95.13.1

Equiano, O. (1789). *The interesting narrative of the life of Olaudah Equiano, Or Gustavus Vassa, the African written by himself.* Retrieved from http://www.gutenberg.org/files/15399/15399-h/15399-h.htm

Falconbridge, A. (1792). *An account of the slave trade from the coast of Africa.* Retrieved from https://archive.org/details/accountofslavetr00falc

Falconer, E. (ca. 1930s). Interview. Library of Congress, Washington, D.C. Retrieved from http://www.loc.gov/teachers/classroommaterials/presentationsandactivities/presentations/timeline/civilwar/freedmen/emmafal.html

Federal Art Project. (ca. 1936). *Keep your fire escapes clear.* Library of Congress, Washington, D.C. Retrieved from http://www.loc.gov/pictures/resource/ds.05007/

Federal Art Project. (ca. 1942). *Save scrap for victory.* Library of Congress, Washington, D.C. Retrieved from http://www.loc.gov/pictures/resource/cph.3f05676/

First Reconstruction Act. (1867, March 2). [Retrieved from http://teachingamericanhistory.org/library/index.asp?document=1920

The first vote. (1867, Nov. 16). *Harper's Weekly.* Retrieved from http://blackhistory.harpweek.com/7Illustrations/Reconstruction/TheFirstVote.htm

Forsyth, J. (1830, April 15). Speech to Congress. Library of Congress, Washington, D.C. Retrieved from http://memory.loc.gov/cgiin/ampage?collId=llrd&fileName=008/llrd008.db&recNum=346

Franklin, B. (1782, Sept). *Information to Those Who Would Remove to America.* The Founders' Constitution, University of Chicago Press: Chicago, IL. Retrieved from http://press-pubs.uchicago.edu/founders/documents/v1ch15s27.html

Galusha, A. M. (1849, April 3). Correspondence. Center for Lowell History Collection, University of Massachusetts, Lowell, MA. Retrieved from http://libweb.uml.edu/clh/All/gal01.htm

Gardner. A. (1863, Nov. 19). *Dedication ceremonies at the Soldiers' National Cemetery, Gettysburg, Pennsylvania.* Library of Congress, Washington, D.C. Retrieved from http://www.loc.gov/pictures/resource/ppmsca.17807/

Gast, J. (1872). *American progress.* Library of Congress, Washington, D.C. Retrieved from http://www.loc.gov/pictures/resource/cph.3b49232/

Gerwin, D., & Zevin, J. (2011). *Teaching U.S. history as mystery.* New York, NY: Routledge.

Girl at loom. (n.d.). Center for Lowell History Collection, University of Massachusetts, Lowell, MA. Retrieved from http://libweb.uml.edu/clh/All/mgi01.htm

Gottlob, F. (1919). *Remember!* Library of Congress, Washington, D.C. Retrieved from http://www.loc.gov/pictures/resource/cph.3f03992/

The Great Law: Pennsylvania Charter. (1976). In G. M. Beckman (Ed.) (1976). *The statutes at large of Pennsylvania in the time of William Penn, Volume I, 1680–1700.* New York, NY: Vantage Press. Retrieved from http://tinyurl.com/nezrgxo [Original work published in 1682]

Group of slaves on parade, Fort Augusta. (1857). Virginia Foundation for the Humanities and University of Virginia Library, Charlottesville, VA. Retrieved from http://hitchcock.itc.virginia.edu/SlaveTrade/collection/large/iln595d.JPG

Hakluyt, R. (1584). *Discourse of western planting.* Internet Archives. Retrieved from https://archive.org/details/cihm_07386

Hariot, T. (1590). *A brief and true report of the new found land of Virginia.* University of Virginia, Charlottesville, VA. Retrieved from http://etext.lib.virginia.edu/etcbin/jamestown-browsemod?id=J1009

Help to catch Huns. Victory bonds shorten the war. (1918). Library of Congress, Washington, D.C. Retrieved from http://www.loc.gov/pictures/resource/cph.3g12180/

Herczog, M. (2013). The college, career, and civic life (C3) framework for social studies: A watershed moment for social studies. In National Council for the Social Studies, *Social studies for the next generation* (pp. vii–x). Silver Spring, MD: National Council for the Social Studies.

Hine, L. (1908a, Aug.). *Glass works. Midnight. Indiana.* Library of Congress, Washington, D.C. Retrieved from http://www.loc.gov/pictures/resource/nclc.01151/

Hine, L. (1908b, Oct.). *Blower and mold boy, Seneca Glass Works, Morgantown, W. Va.* Library of Congress, Washington, D.C. Retrieved from http://www.loc.gov/pictures/resource/nclc.01185/?co=nclc

Hine, L. (1908c, Oct.). *"Carrying in boy" at the Lehr Glass Factory, Grafton, W. Va.* Library of Congress, Washington, D.C. Retrieved from http://www.loc.gov/pictures/resource/nclc.01177/

Hine, L. (1908d, Oct.). *Citizens' Glass Co., Evansville, Ind.* Library of Congress, Washington, D.C. Retrieved from http://www.loc.gov/pictures/resource/nclc.01204/

Hine, L. (1908e, Oct.). *Drivers and trappers going home: Barnesville Mine.* Library of Congress, Washington, D.C. Retrieved from http://www.loc.gov/pictures/item/ncl2004000212/PP/

Hine, L. (1908f, Oct.). *Lincoln Cotton Mill, Evansville, Ind. Girl at slubber.* Library of Congress, Washington, D.C. Retrieved from http://www.loc.gov/pictures/resource/nclc.01330/

Hine, L. (1908g, Oct.). *Mannington Glass Works.* Library of Congress, Washington, D.C. Retrieved from http://www.loc.gov/pictures/resource/nclc.01190/

Hine, L. (1908h, Nov.). *Girls running warping machines in Loray mill, Gastonia, N.C.* Library of Congress, Washington, D.C. Retrieved from http://www.loc.gov/pictures/resource/nclc.01342/

Historic Jamestown. (n.d.a). *Growth of Jamestown.* Jamestown Rediscovery Collection, Jamestown, VA. Retrieved from http://apva.org/rediscovery/page.php?page_id=193

Historic Jamestown. (n.d.b). *Original settlers and occupations.* Jamestown Rediscovery Collection, Jamestown, VA. Retrieved from http://apva.org/rediscovery/page.php?page_id=31

Holyoke, E. (1967). The testimony of Harvard College against George Whitefield. In A. Heimert and P. Miller (Eds.), *The Great Awakening: Documents illustrating the crisis and its consequences* (pp. 340–353). New York, NY: The Bobbs-Merrill Company. [Original work published 1744, Dec. 28]

Homann, J. B. (1759). *Virginia, Marylandia et Carolina in America septentrionaliBritannorum.* Library of Congress, Washington, D.C. Retrieved from http://www.loc.gov/item/73691852/

Homer, W. (n.d.) *Bobbin girl.* Center for Lowell History Collection, University of Massachusetts, Lowell, MA. Retrieved from http://libweb.uml.edu/clh/All/mgi04.htm

Hunter, L. (1938). I'd rather not be on relief. Library of Congress, Washington, D.C. Retrieved from http://www.loc.gov/teachers/classroommaterials/primarysourcesets/dust-bowl-migration/pdf/relief.pdf

Jackson, A. (1830). Second annual message to Congress. Library of Congress, Washington, D.C. Retrieved from http://memory.loc.gov/cgi-bin/ampage?collId=llhj&fileName=024/llhj024.db&recNum=24

James Plantation Freedmen's Bureau school. (ca. 1868, October). North Carolina State University History Department, Raleigh, NC. Retrieved from http://history.ncsu.edu/projects/cwnc/items/show/180

King James I. (1606, April 10). *The First Charter of Virginia.* Yale Law School, Lillian Goldman Law Library, New Haven, CT. Retrieved from http://avalon.law.yale.edu/17th_century/va01.asp

Jay, J. (1787, Oct. 31). *Federalist 2: Concerning Dangers from Foreign Force and Influence For the Independent Journal.* Yale Law School, Lillian Goldman Law Library, New Haven, CT. Retrieved from http://avalon.law.yale.edu/18th_century/fed02.asp

Jefferson, T. (1803, June 20). Correspondence [Thomas Jefferson writing to Meriwether Lewis]. In Gawalt, G. W. (Ed.), *Rivers, Edens, Empires: Lewis & Clark and the Revealing of America Collection.* Library of

Congress, Washington, D.C. Retrieved from http://www.loc.gov/exhibits/lewisandclark/transcript57.html

Johnson, A. (1867, March 2). Veto for the First Reconstruction Act. Digital History. Retrieved from http://www.digitalhistory.uh.edu/exhibits/reconstruction/section4/section4_10veto.html

King, Jr., M. L. (1963, Aug. 28). I have a dream. National Archives, Washington, D.C. Retrieved from http://www.archives.gov/press/exhibits/dream-speech.pdf

Lange, D. (1935). *Oklahoma dust bowl refugees. San Fernando, California.* Library of Congress, Washington, D.C. Retrieved from http://www.loc.gov/pictures/resource/fsa.8b27316/

Lange, D. (1936a). *Destitute pea pickers in California. Mother of seven children.* Library of Congress, Washington, D.C. Retrieved from http://www.loc.gov/pictures/resource/fsa.8b29516/

Lange, D. (1936b). *Example of self-resettlement in California.* Library of Congress, Washington, D.C. Retrieved from http://www.loc.gov/pictures/resource/fsa.8b38486/

Lange, D. (1936c). *Migrant agricultural worker's family.* Library of Congress, Washington, D.C. Retrieved from http://www.loc.gov/pictures/resource/ppmsca.03054/

Lawes Divine, Morall, and Martiall. (1610–1611). Jamestown Learning Resources Collection, Jamestown Settlement, Jamestown, VA. Retrieved from http://www.historyisfun.org/pdf/Laws-at-Jamestown/Lawes_Divine_Morall_and_Martiall.pdf

Leffler, W. K. (1963, August 28). *Civil Rights March on Washington D.C.* Library of Congress, Washington, D.C. Retrieved from http://www.loc.gov/pictures/resource/ppmsca.03128/

Leutze, E. (1862). *Westward the course of empire takes its way.* Architect of the Capitol, Washington, D.C. Retrieved from http://www.aoc.gov/capitol-hill/other-paintings-and-murals/westward-course-empire-takes-its-way

Lincoln, A. (1863). Gettysburg address. National Archives, Washington, D.C. Retrieved from http://www.ourdocuments.gov/doc.php?doc=36&page=transcript

Lincoln, A. (1865, March 14). Second inaugural address. Library of Congress, Washington, D.C. Retrieved from http://www.ourdocuments.gov/doc.php?flash=true&doc=38

Lincoln's Gettysburg Address, Gettysburg. (1863). Library of Congress, Washington, D.C. Retrieved from http://www.loc.gov/pictures/item/2012648250/

Lowell carpet mills. (1850). Center for Lowell History Collection, University of Massachusetts, Lowell, MA. Retrieved from http://libweb.uml.edu/clh/All/mi10.htm

Mayflower Compact. (1620). The Avalon Project Collection, Yale Law School, Lillian Goldman Law Library. New Haven, CT. Retrieved from http://avalon.law.yale.edu/17th_century/mayflower.asp

McCutcheon, J. T. (1914). What the United States has fought for. Retrieved from https://upload.wikimedia.org/wikipedia/commons/e/e4/Free_from_Spanish.jpg

McCutcheon, J. (ca. 1931). A wise economist asks a question. *Chicago Tribune.* Library of Congress, Washington, D.C. Retrieved from http://www.loc.gov/pictures/item/acd1996005778/PP/

Meynell, F. (1845). *Hold of Brazilian slave ship, 1845.* Virginia Foundation for the Humanities and University of Virginia Library, Charlottesville, VA. Retrieved from http://hitchcock.itc.virginia.edu/SlaveTrade/collection/large/E029.JPG

Miyatake, A. (n.d.). Interview by Karen Ishizuka. Japanese American National Museum, Los Angeles, CA. Retrieved from http://www.janm.org/exhibits/breed/interv.htm

Morgan, P. G. (1918). *Keep this hand of mercy at its work.* Library of Congress, Washington, D.C. Retrieved from http://www.loc.gov/pictures/resource/cph.3g07762/

Mueller, H. (1919). *Adventure and action: Enlist in the field artillery, U.S. Army.* Library of Congress, Washington, D.C. Retrieved from http://www.loc.gov/pictures/resource/cph.3g07577/

Mydans, C. (1935). *CCC (Civilian Conservation Corps) workers, Prince George's County, Maryland.* Library of Congress, Washington, D.C. Retrieved from http://www.loc.gov/pictures/resource/fsa.8a00073/

Nast, T. (1864, Dec. 31). The Union Christmas dinner. *Harper's Weekly.* Retrieved from http://www.harpweek.com/09Cartoon/BrowseByDateCartoon.asp?Month=December&Date=31

Nast, T. (1869, Nov. 20). Uncle Sam's Thanksgiving dinner. *Harper's Weekly.* Retrieved from http://www.harpweek.com/09Cartoon/BrowseByDateCartoon.asp?Month=November&Date=22

Nast, T. (1871, Feb. 18). The Chinese question. *Harper's Weekly.* Retrieved from http://www.harpweek.com/09Cartoon/BrowseByDateCartoon.asp?Month=February&Date=18

Nast, T. (1874, Oct. 24). Worse than slavery. *Harper's Weekly.* Retrieved from http://blackhistory.harpweek.com/7Illustrations/Reconstruction/UnionAsItWas.htm

National Center for History in the Schools. (n.d.). *United States history content standards for grades 5-12.* Retrieved from http://www.nchs.ucla.edu/history-standards/us-history-content-standards

National Council for the Social Studies. (2013). *The College, Career, and Civic Life (C3) Framework for Social Studies State Standards: Guidance for enhancing the rigor of K–12 civics, economics, geography, and history.* Silver Spring, MD: Author.

National Geographic. (n.d.a). *Lewis and Clark's expedition supplies.* Retrieved from http://www.nationalgeographic.com/lewisandclark/resources.html

National Geographic. (n.d.b) Yosemite National Park photos. Retrieved from http://travel.nationalgeographic.com/travel/national-parks/yosemite-photos/

National Governors Association Center for Best Practices, & Council of Chief State School Officers. (2010). *Common Core State Standards for English Language Arts.* Washington, D.C.: Author.

National Park Service. (n.d.a). Grand Tetons: Photo Gallery. Retrieved from http://www.nps.gov/grte/photosmultimedia/photogallery.htm

National Park Service. (n.d.b). Jim Crow laws. Retrieved from http://www.nps.gov/malu/forteachers/jim_crow_laws.htm

National Park Service. (n.d.c). Yellowstone: Photo Gallery. Retrieved from http://www.nps.gov/yell/photosmultimedia/photogallery.htm

Negro laborers at Alexandria near coal wharf. (ca. 1860–1865). National Archives, Washington, D.C. Retrieved from http://docsteach.org/documents/524820/detail?mode=browse&menu=closed&type%5B%5D=image&sortBy=era&page=18

A new method of macarony making, as practised at Boston. (1774). Library of Congress, Washington, D.C. Retrieved from http://www.loc.gov/pictures/resource/cph.3a45583/

O'Sullivan, J. L. (1839). *The Great Nation of Futurity.* Making of American, Cornell University. Retrieved from http://digital.library.cornell.edu/cgi/t/text/text-idx?c=usde;idno=usde0006-4

Oursel, P. (n.d.). *Top deck of French slave ship.* Virginia Foundation for the Humanities and University of Virginia Library, Charlottesville, VA. Retrieved from http://hitchcock.itc.virginia.edu/SlaveTrade/collection/large/E009.JPG

Paine, T. (1776). *Common sense.* Retrieved from http://www.gutenberg.org/files/147/147-h/147-h.htm

Palmer, F. (ca. 1868). *Across the continent: Westward the course of empire takes its way.* Library of Congress, Washington, D.C. Retrieved from http://www.loc.gov/pictures/resource/cph.3f03757/

Parker, C. (1917). *Little Americans do your bit.* Library of Congress, Washington, D.C. Retrieved from http://www.loc.gov/pictures/resource/cph.3g10218/

Percy, G. (1624). *A true relation of the proceedings and occurances of moment which have happened in Virginia . . . .* Retrieved from http://nationalhumanitiescenter.org/pds/amerbegin/settlement/text2/JamestownPercyRelation.pdf

Philadelphia Press. (1898). Ten thousand miles from tip to tip. Retrieved from http://commons.wikimedia.org/wiki/File:10kMiles.JPG

President Truman wipes out segregation in armed forces. (1948, July 31). *Chicago Defender.* Library of Congress, Washington, D.C. Retrieved from http://www.loc.gov/exhibits/odyssey/archive/09/0902001r.jpg

Public Broadcasting Service. (n.d.a). Propaganda techniques. Retrieved from http://www-tc.pbs.org/weta/reportingamericaatwar/teachers/pdf/propaganda.pdf

Public Broadcasting Service. (n.d.b). The War Project: Witnesses on the Homefront Collection. Retrieved from http://www.pbs.org/thewar/the_witnesses_homefront.htm

Pughe, J. S. (1900). "Hurrah! The country is saved again!" Library of Congress, Washington, D.C., Retrieved from http://www.loc.gov/pictures/resource/ppmsca.25473/

Raleigh. H. (ca. 1918). *Halt the Hun.* Library of Congress, Washington, D.C. Retrieved from http://www.loc.gov/pictures/resource/cph.3b48556/

Rapp, O. J. (1964). *President Johnson signs the Civil Rights Act of 1964.* Lyndon B. Johnson Presidential Library, Austin, TX. Retrieved from http://www.lbjlibrary.net/collections/photo-archive.html

Rentschler, F. (1938). *This is an adult world, its problems are up to you!* Library of Congress, Washington, D.C. Retrieved from http://www.loc.gov/pictures/resource/cph.3f05422/

The repeal, or the funeral of Miss Ame=Stamp. (n.d.). Library of Congress, Washington, D.C. Retrieved from http://www.loc.gov/pictures/resource/ppmsca.15709/

Revere, P. (1770). *The bloody massacre perpetrated in King Street Boston on March 5th, 1770 by a party of the 29th Regt.* Library of Congress, Washington, D.C. Retrieved by http://www.loc.gov/pictures/resource/ppmsca.01657/

Rice, S., (1845, Feb. 23). Correspondence. Center for Lowell History Collection, University of Massachusetts, Lowell, MA. Retrieved from http://libweb.uml.edu/clh/All/ric03.htm

Riis, J. (1890). *How the other half lives: Studies among the tenements of New York.* Retrieved from http://ebooks.gutenberg.us/WorldeBookLibrary.com/otherhalf.htm

Ritchie, A. H. (ca. 1868). *Sherman's march to the sea.* Library of Congress, Washington, D.C. Retrieved from http://www.loc.gov/pictures/resource/ppmsca.09326/

The road to dividends. (ca 1913). Library of Congress, Washington, D.C. Retrieved from http://www.loc.gov/pictures/resource/nclc.02853/

Robertson, F. (ca. 1940). Why we come to Californy. Library of Congress, Washington, D.C. Retrieved from http://www.loc.gov/teachers/classroom materials/primarysourcesets/dust-bowl-migration/pdf/californy.pdf

Rogers, W. (1883, April 28). The balance of trade with Great Britain seems to still be against us. *Harper's Weekly.* Retrieved from http://www.harpweek.com/09Cartoon/BrowseByDateCartoon.asp?Month=April&Date=28

Ronald Martin, Robert Patterson, and Mark Martin stage sit-down strike after being refused service at a F.W. Woolworth luncheon counter, Greensboro, N.C. (1960). Retrieved from http://www.loc.gov/exhibits/odyssey/archive/09/0909001r.jpg

Ross, J. (1836, September 28). Cherokee Nation's Letter to the Senate and House of Representatives. Retrieved from http://historymatters.gmu.edu/d/6598/

Roosevelt, F. D. (1942, April 28). Radio Address. Miller Center, University of Virginia. Retrieved from http://millercenter.org/president/speeches/speech-3327

Ruins of Atlanta, GA, 1864. (1864). National Archives, Washington, D.C. Retrieved from http://docsteach.org/documents/528865/detail

Sayer, R., & Bennett, J. (1774, Oct. 31). The Bostonians paying the excise man, or tarring and feathering. Library of Congress, Washington, D.C. Retrieved from http://www.loc.gov/pictures/resource/cph.3a11950/

Schile, H. (1876). *1776, Centennial International Exhibition, 1876, history of the United States.* Library of Congress, Washington, D. C. Retrieved from http://www.loc.gov/pictures/item/2003656440/

Scieszka, J. (1989). *The true story of the three little pigs.* New York, NY: Puffin Books.

Segregation in schools is outlawed. (1954, May 17). *The Russell Daily News.* Library of Congress, Washington, D.C. Retrieved from http://www.loc.gov/exhibits/brown/brown-brown.html

Sheer, B. (1936). *Better housing: The solution to infant mortality in the slums.* Library of Congress, Washington, D.C. Retrieved from http://www.loc.gov/pictures/resource/cph.3f05647/

Shipping slaves through the surf, West African coast. A cruiser signalled in sight. (n.d.) Virginia Foundation for the Humanities and University of Virginia Library, Charlottesville, VA. Retrieved from http://hitchcock.itc.virginia.edu/SlaveTrade/collection/large/CMI-surf.JPG

Shurtleff, W. (1967). Letter to those who refuse to admit Whitefield. In A. Heimert and P. Miller (Eds.), *The Great Awakening: Documents illustrating the crisis and its consequences* (pp. 354–363). New York, NY: The Bobbs-Merrill Company. [Original work published in 1745]

Smith, J. (1612). *A map of Virginia: With a description of the country, the commodities, people, government and religion.* Retrieved from http://www.virtualjamestown.org/jsmap_large.html

Smith, J. (1967). Whitefield's character and preaching. In A. Heimert and P. Miller (Eds.), *The Great Awakening: Documents illustrating the crisis and its consequences* (pp. 62–69). New York, NY: The Bobbs-Merrill Company. [Original work published in 1740]

South Carolina government carpenter's shops. (n.d.). National Archives, Washington, D.C. Retrieved from http://www.archives.gov/global-pages/larger-image.html?i=/research/african-americans/freedmens-bureau/images/carpenters-shop-l.jpg&c=/research/african-americans/freedmens-bureau/images/carpenters-shop.caption.html

Spinning frame with young woman. (n.d.) University of Massachusetts, Lowell, MA. Retrieved from http://libweb.uml.edu/clh/All/mgi02.htm

Sprague, P. (1830, April 17). Speech to Congress. Library of Congress, Washington, D.C. Retrieved from http://memory.loc.gov/cgi-bin/ampage?collId=llrd&fileName=008/llrd008.db&recNum=4

Steinlen. T. (1916). *Save Serbia our ally.* Library of Congress, Washington, D.C. Retrieved from http://www.loc.gov/pictures/resource/cph.3f03989/

Stowage of the British slave ship Brookes under the regulated slave trade. (1790). Virginia Foundation for the Humanities and University of Virginia Library, Charlottesville, VA. Retrieved from http://hitchcock.itc.virginia.edu/SlaveTrade/collection/large/E014.JPG

Sullivan, M. (ca. 1930s). Sunny California. Library of Congress, Washington, D.C. Retrieved from http://www.loc.gov/teachers/lyrical/songs/docs/california_trans.pdf

Tasker, W. (ca. 1942). *Service on the homefront.* Library of Congress, Washington, D.C. Retrieved from http://www.loc.gov/pictures/resource/cph.3b49007/

Time table of the Lowell Mills. (1851). Center for Lowell History Collection, University of Massachusetts, Lowell, MA. Retrieved from http://libweb.uml.edu/clh/All/doc02.htm

Tisdale, E. (1795). The Tory's day of judgment. Library of Congress, Washington, D.C. Retrieved from http://www.loc.gov/pictures/resource/cph.3a10349/

United States Census Bureau. (1860). Census of 1860. Retrieved from https://www.census.gov/history/www/through_the_decades/overview/1860.html

U.S. Office of War Information. (1943, March). *Do with less.* Library of Congress, Washington, D.C. Retrieved from http://www.loc.gov/pictures/resource/fsa.8b06175/

Vachon, J. (1938a). *Railroad station, Manchester, Georgia.* Retrieved from http://www.loc.gov/pictures/item/fsa1997003449/PP

Vachon, J. (1938b). *Drinking fountain on the country courthouse lawn.* Retrieved from http://www.locl.gov/pictures/item/fsa1997003218/PP/

Vanderlyn, J. (1847). *Landing of Columbus.* Architect of the Capitol Historic Rotunda Paintings Collection, Washington, D.C. Retrieved from http://www.aoc.gov/capitol-hill/historic-rotunda-paintings/landing-columbus

Visscher, N. (1690). *Novi Belgii Novæque Angliæ: nec non partis Virginiæ tabula multis in locis emendata.* Library of Congress, Washington, D.C. Retrieved from http://www.loc.gov/item/97683561/

War gardens for victory. (ca. 1942). Library of Congress, Washington, D.C. Retrieved from http://www.loc.gov/pictures/resource/cph.3g04436/

Washington, G. (1796). Farewell address. National Archives, Washington, D.C. Retrieved from http://www.ourdocuments.gov/doc.php?doc=15

"What did you do in the war, Grandma?" Oral Histories of Rhode Island Women in WWII. (1995). Interviews by Honors English students at South Kingstown High School. Retrieved from http://cds.library.brown.edu/projects/WWII_Women/tocCS.html

Whitehead. W. (1918). *Stand by the boys in the trenches—mine more coal.* Library of Congress, Washington, D.C. Retrieved from http://www.loc.gov/pictures/resource/cph.3g07924/

Wineburg, S., Martin, D., & Monte-Sano, C. (2013). *Reading like a historian: Teaching literacy in middle & high school history classrooms.* New York, NY: Teachers College Press.

Wolcott, M. P. (1939a). *Beale Street, Memphis, Tennessee.* Retrieved from http://www.loc.gov/pictures/item/fsa1998013763/PP/

Wolcott, M. P. (1939b). *Negro going in colored entrance of movie house on Saturday afternoon, Belzoni, Mississippi Delta, Mississippi.* Retrieved from http://www.loc.gov/pictures/item/fsa1998013484/PP/

Wolfe, M. A. (1877, July 28) Untitled. *Harper's Weekly.* Retrieved from http://www.harpweek.com/09Cartoon/BrowseByDateCartoon.asp?Month=July&Date=28

Woman fingerprinted. Mrs. Rosa Parks, Negro seamstress, whose refusal to move to the back of a bus touched off the bus boycott in Montgomery, Ala. (1956). Library of Congress, Washington, D.C. Retrieved from http://www.loc.gov/pictures/item/94500293/?sid=61c69742c46cd2d89737b98496366177

Yolen, J. (1992). *Encounter.* New York, NY: Harcourt.

ABOUT THE AUTHORS

Jana Kirchner, Ph.D., is an assistant professor in the School of Teacher Education at Western Kentucky University. She has 25 years of experience in education, which includes being a Social Studies Consultant/Teaching American History grant coordinator, an ACT Quality Core facilitator, and a high school English and social studies teacher. She earned her Ph.D. in educational leadership, with an emphasis in curriculum and instruction, from the University of Louisville. She has provided professional development, coached teachers, presented at state and national conferences, and written articles and book chapters on social studies, content literacy, differentiation, and effective teaching strategies.

Andrew McMichael, Ph.D., is an associate professor of history and the assistant dean in the Potter College of Arts & Letters at Western Kentucky University. Prior to earning his Ph.D. in American history from Vanderbilt University in 2000, he taught high school and gained teaching experience in kindergarten, third-, and fifth-grade classrooms. His current work focuses on fostering collaborations between content and pedagogical experts in the field of teacher training. He visits more than a dozen elementary school classrooms each year, delivering many of the lessons found in this volume.

COMMON CORE STATE STANDARDS ALIGNMENT

Chapter	Common Core State Standards
Chapter 2	CCSS.ELA-Literacy.RH.6-8.1: Cite specific textual evidence to support analysis of primary and secondary sources. CCSS.ELA-Literacy.RH.6-8.8: Distinguish among fact, opinion, and reasoned judgment in a text.
Chapter 3	CCSS.ELA-Literacy.RH.6-8.2: Determine the central ideas or information of a primary or secondary source; provide an accurate summary of the source distinct from prior knowledge or opinions. CCSS.ELA-Literacy.RH.6-8.1: Cite specific textual evidence to support analysis of primary and secondary sources.
Chapter 4	CCSS.ELA-Literacy.RH.6-8.2: Determine the central ideas or information of a primary or secondary source; provide an accurate summary of the source distinct from prior knowledge or opinions. CCSS.ELA-Literacy.RH.6-8.1: Cite specific textual evidence to support analysis of primary and secondary sources. CCSS.ELA-Literacy.RH.6-8.7: Integrate visual information (e.g., in charts, graphs, photographs, videos, or maps) with other information in print and digital texts.
Chapter 5	CCSS.ELA-Literacy.RH.6-8.5: Describe how a text presents information (e.g., sequentially, comparatively, causally). CCSS.ELA-Literacy.RH.6-8.2: Determine the central ideas or information of a primary or secondary source; provide an accurate summary of the source distinct from prior knowledge or opinions. CCSS.ELA-Literacy.RH.6-8.1: Cite specific textual evidence to support analysis of primary and secondary sources.
Chapter 6	CCSS.ELA-Literacy.RH.6.8.4: Determine the meaning of words and phrases as they are used in a text, including vocabulary specific to domains related to history/social studies. CCSS.ELA-Literacy.RH.6-8.5: Describe how a text presents information (e.g., sequentially, comparatively, causally). CCSS.ELA-Literacy.RH.6-8.2: Determine the central ideas or information of a primary or secondary source; provide an accurate summary of the source distinct from prior knowledge or opinions.

Chapter	Common Core State Standards
Chapter 7	CCSS.ELA-Literacy.RH.6-8.2: Determine the central ideas or information of a primary or secondary source; provide an accurate summary of the source distinct from prior knowledge or opinions. CCSS.ELA-Literacy.RH.6-8.1: Cite specific textual evidence to support analysis of primary and secondary sources.
Chapter 8	CCSS.ELA-Literacy.RH.6-8.1: Cite specific textual evidence to support analysis of primary and secondary sources. CCSS.ELA-Literacy.RH.6-8.6: Identify aspects of a text that reveal an author's point of view or purpose (e.g., loaded language, inclusion or avoidance of particular facts). CCSS.ELA-Literacy.RH.6-8.7: Integrate visual information (e.g., in charts, graphs, photographs, videos, or maps) with other information in print and digital texts.
Chapter 9	CCSS.ELA-Literacy.RH.6-8.7: Integrate visual information (e.g., in charts, graphs, photographs, videos, or maps) with other information in print and digital texts. CCSS.ELA-Literacy.RH.6-8.2: Determine the central ideas or information of a primary or secondary source; provide an accurate summary of the source distinct from prior knowledge or opinions.
Chapter 10	CCSS.ELA-Literacy.RH.6-8.1: Cite specific textual evidence to support analysis of primary and secondary sources. CCSS.ELA-Literacy.RH.6-8.6: Identify aspects of a text that reveal an author's point of view or purpose (e.g., loaded language, inclusion or avoidance of particular facts). CCSS.ELA-Literacy.RH.6-8.7: Integrate visual information (e.g., in charts, graphs, photographs, videos, or maps) with other information in print and digital texts.
Chapter 11	CCSS.ELA-Literacy.RH.6-8.7: Integrate visual information (e.g., in charts, graphs, photographs, videos, or maps) with other information in print and digital texts. CCSS.ELA-Literacy.RH.6-8.1: Cite specific textual evidence to support analysis of primary and secondary sources.
Chapter 12	CCSS.ELA-Literacy.RH.6-8.1: Cite specific textual evidence to support analysis of primary and secondary sources. CCSS.ELA-Literacy.RH.6-8.2: Determine the central ideas or information of a primary or secondary source; provide an accurate summary of the source distinct from prior knowledge or opinions. CCSS.ELA-Literacy.RH.6-8.7: Integrate visual information (e.g., in charts, graphs, photographs, videos, or maps) with other information in print and digital texts.

Chapter	Common Core State Standards
Chapter 13	CCSS.ELA-Literacy.RH.6-8.7: Integrate visual information (e.g., in charts, graphs, photographs, videos, or maps) with other information in print and digital texts. CCSS.ELA-Literacy.RH.6-8.2: Determine the central ideas or information of a primary or secondary source; provide an accurate summary of the source distinct from prior knowledge or opinions. CCSS.ELA-Literacy.RH.6-8.6: Identify aspects of a text that reveal an author's point of view or purpose (e.g., loaded language, inclusion or avoidance of particular facts).